OUT OF
COMMISSION

GETTING EVERY CHRISTIAN
BACK *to the*
GREAT COMMISSION

PAUL CHAPPELL

First published in 2014 by Striving Together Publications, a ministry of Lancaster Baptist Church, Lancaster, CA 93535. Striving Together Publications is committed to providing tried, trusted, and proven books that will further equip local churches to carry out the Great Commission. Your comments and suggestions are valued.

Striving Together Publications
4020 E. Lancaster Blvd.
Lancaster, CA 93535
800.201.7748

Cover design by Andrew Jones
Layout by Craig Parker
Writing assistance by Monica Bass
Special thanks to our proofreaders.

The author and publication team have given every effort to give proper credit to quotes and thoughts that are not original with the author. It is not our intent to claim originality with any quote or thought that could not readily be tied to an original source.

ISBN 978-1-59894-255-2

Printed in the United States of America

DEDICATION

To my mother, Maxine Chappell.

I first learned to share the gospel with others by
going door-to-door soulwinning with my mom
when I was eight years old. She rarely misses a week
when she finds time to witness and finds people with
whom to share the gospel. Even now as she battles
Alzheimer's, she speaks passionately for Christ in her
daily life and in her soulwinning times.

ACKNOWLEDGEMENTS

This book is a result of the efforts of many people, and I am thankful for their generous contributions.

First, thank you, Terrie, for your love and faithfulness to me. Thank you for sharing over thirty-two years of gospel ministry with me and for being a personal soulwinner. Thank you for being my lifelong partner and my favorite soulwinning partner.

Thank you, Lancaster Baptist Church family, for your obedience to the Great Commission, your diligence in loving, welcoming, and discipling new Christians, and your faithfulness in reaching into our community with the gospel of Jesus Christ.

I also want to thank a team of people who brought this manuscript to completion. Thank you, Monica Bass, for your writing assistance in making this book a reality. Thank you, Danielle Mordh, Tobi England, and Gary Spaeth, for your editorial review and suggestions. And thank you to our entire Striving Together Publications team and our volunteer team of proofreaders for your detailed efforts in preparing this manuscript for press.

Finally, I want to thank a few pastor friends who reviewed this manuscript. Thank you, Pastor Tim Rasmussen, Pastor Troy Dorrell, Pastor Shane Lewis, and Dr. R.B. Ouellette, for your encouragement and feedback. I appreciate your friendship!

CONTENTS

F O R E W O R D

During the weekly opportunities God gives me to preach in other churches, I usually shake hands at the door after the service. I regularly ask those I am meeting, "How long have you been in this church?" I then ask if they were saved through the ministries of the church or if they were already saved when they began to come. It encourages me to meet so many whose lives have been changed by the gospel.

I never meet a larger percentage of people who were saved through the ministry of their local church than I do when I preach at Lancaster Baptist Church. Dr. Paul Chappell is a personal soulwinner. In spite of the immense responsibility he has and the intense schedule he maintains, he makes time on a weekly basis to knock on doors and to set up appointments and tell people the gospel of Jesus Christ. I have met those he has led to Christ. I have seen those he has won obey the Lord in baptism, grow in grace, and become longtime, faithful members of the local church.

Some books on soulwinning are practical—they present nuts and bolts, the how-to-do-it details. This book is extremely practical.

Some books on soulwinning are principled—they deal with the concept, the Bible command, and the moral responsibility those of us who know God have to tell those who don't know God how they may know Him. This book is extremely principled and biblical. It thoroughly presents the doctrine of soulwinning.

But there is a third dimension of this book. It is practical, it is principled, but it is also passionate. Soulwinning is at the heart of the life and ministry of Dr. Paul Chappell. It is at the heart of the Lancaster Baptist Church.

There are places where soulwinning is a lost art. There are churches and preachers who give lip service to soulwinning but no life service. The Lancaster Baptist Church is not such a church, and Dr. Paul Chappell is not such a preacher. For twenty-eight years, soulwinning has been "the main thing" for Dr. Chappell and the church he leads.

This book is a wonderful reminder that soulwinning is not dependant on the climate, the economy, or current events. It does not require large amounts of money or extensive education. It can be practiced by the simple and the sophisticated, the socially adept and the socially awkward. PhDs can be soulwinners...as well as people who never finished the eighth grade.

Soulwinning works because of the "dynamite" of the gospel. It succeeds because of the power of the Holy Spirit. It is neither traditional nor trendy, up to date or outmoded. It is timeless.

Please read carefully this wonderful book. Allow it to influence your thinking and your behavior. More importantly, allow the heart of this book to become your heart. You will find that it is the heart of God.

Dr. R.B. Ouellette
Pastor, First Baptist Church of Bridgeport
Bridgeport, Michigan

INTRODUCTION
ENGINE OVERHAUL

You'd be hard pressed to meet a dedicated Christian who doesn't say the greatest work on Earth is evangelization. After all, we know this is the responsibility Christ gave the church before ascending to Heaven. He commissioned the local church to be His vehicle for delivering the gospel into all the world—a tremendous privilege with tremendous responsibility.

But while all of us give lip service to evangelizing and discipling, the effect of our labor seems woefully behind. Statistics tell us that while the American population grew 9.7 percent from 2000–2010,[1] nationwide church attendance has dropped 2 percent.[2] Although these statistics cover every type of church affiliation, not just gospel-preaching churches, they are indicative of a failure on our part to reach our communities with the gospel. Somewhere there is a disconnect between the priorities we claim and the actions we practice. Something is broken…or maybe just out of commission.

Through over thirty years in ministry, the Lord has given me the privilege of knowing and being mentored by passionate soulwinners. He's allowed me to lead many dear souls to Him personally and to lead a local church that is aggressive in its obedience to saturate our community with the gospel and to disciple new believers in the faith. From my experience and from the testimonies of those led to Christ through personal soulwinners, those discipled through the local church, and those engaged now in the same, I believe the greatest need is for Christians once again to engage in the work Jesus left us to do—telling others the gospel of Jesus Christ.

Every Christian I know would agree with my assessment. But while we agree verbally, our focus and our priorities don't affirm what we say. To be frank, we're distracted today. While millions of people right here in our own country—and billions more around the world—are perishing into a Christ-less eternity, we pour our energies into good projects, but not the best project. We fall into petty squabbles and ridiculous (in comparison) issues of little lasting importance while the greatest work lies neglected.

This is not to say that other issues don't matter—some do, and many discussions are vital. This is not to say the cure for everything is "just to go soulwinning"—it's not. But it is to say that we have lost our focus, have slipped in our priorities, and have disengaged from our greatest mission. While our "engine" is in disrepair, we deliberate at great length on the best way to fix our chipped paint or whether or not we should install cool rims.

But all the while, we neglect the engine. We miss the greatest issue—reaching men and women with the gospel of Christ.

This book is not an attempt to fix a broken engine by refueling it with zeal. No amount of gasoline can power a broken engine, and no amount of zeal can power an out-of-commission Christian. We've seen the products of flesh and zeal, and they are not sufficient.

This book, rather, is an invitation to undergo a serious engine overhaul. In these pages, I invite you to consider with me what it would take to reengage your life and, by way of influence, your church in the Great Commission of Jesus Christ. This book is a call back to focused soulwinning and discipleship. It's a challenge to lift the hood, examine the engine, make needed adjustments, and move forward doing what Christ commissioned us to do.

----

1   Paul Mackun and Steven Wilson, "Population Distribution and Change: 2000 to 2010" (2010 Census Briefs), http://www.census.gov/prod/cen2010/briefs/c2010br-01.pdf.

2   Michael Lipka, "What Surveys Say about Worship Attendance" (Pew Research Center, September 13, 2013), http://www.pewresearch.org/fact-tank/2013/09/13/what-surveys-say-about-worship-attendance-and-why-some-stay-home/.

PART ONE

THE COST OF NEGLECT

ONE
A NEGLECTED MISSION

Remember those chore lists your mom would leave you with as she hurried out the door to an appointment? *You* probably hopped right to it and got your list completed before your mom returned. I didn't always. But those are stories for another time and place (particularly because my mom reads my books).

Mom doesn't leave me chore lists anymore, which I'm sure we'll all agree is an indisputable evidence of my maturity. But a few years ago, I found myself with that nagging unfinished chore list dilemma again. Only this time, it wasn't my mom I was going to answer to; it was my grandmother. And it wasn't a list before she left; it was a truck to repair before she returned.

When my granddad died, my grandmother gave me his 1988 brown Ford truck. For me, this was an invaluable gift. The truck holds memories of time I got to spend with one of the greatest men I've known. If you knew my granddad, you would agree.

The only problem was that the truck needed repairs, and I didn't have time immediately to get it fixed. So it sat in my back yard—a model of memories. I was happy with the arrangement. Just seeing the truck from time to time reminded me of Granddad and the many memories I shared with him in the truck.

But then something happened that changed the way I looked at the model truck in my backyard. Grandmother planned a visit to California.

I love my grandmother and was, of course, excited for her to come—except for one thing. The truck. Looking at the truck through her eyes, I realized how sorely it had deteriorated. What I had enjoyed as a shiny model of memories was actually looking more like a neglected old pickup.

So I did what any kid would do before his mother comes home to see his uncompleted list. I hid it. Yes, I moved the truck to my married son's house so Grandmother wouldn't see it.

The pastor of our church's Spanish ministry helped me get the truck moved. As we finished, I began to feel a bit of remorse and wondered aloud what it would take to get the truck restored. I even asked him if he knew any mechanics who would be equal to the task. He said he did and would give me their contact information.

A few days later, Grandmother came. We had a great time together. And then she left. And I forgot all about the truck. Out of sight, out of mind.

Some months later, I celebrated my birthday. Actually, the Spanish department of our church celebrated my birthday—in a big way. Weeks earlier, they had taken up an offering to pay for the restoration of Granddad's truck. With the truck safely hidden from my sight at my son's house, they had been able to haul it off and do serious work on it. A mechanic in our church helped, working on the engine during his off time for a few weeks. They had the seats reupholstered, bought new tires, and added shiny rims.

When the Spanish department presented Granddad's restored truck to me after the morning service one Sunday, I could hardly believe my eyes. What a gift! Their careful work had removed the evidences of neglect. Granddad would have been proud.

The old, out-of-commission truck is an example of the cost of neglect. What had once been a useable truck was put out of commission simply through neglect.

It is also an example of the possibility of repair. The neglect could be reversed! Now, I use the truck, and my own grandson, Camden, is building memories of his own of time with *his* Papa as we take it out on drives together.

Like my granddad's truck, many local churches are deteriorating through neglect of their purpose. Christ gave us a mission—we could call it a chore list, but it's far bigger than that. It is our solemn responsibility. That mission is to evangelize the world.

But we've neglected our duty. Sat down on the job. Forgotten our purpose.

The result? We're out of commission.

I'm not talking in terms of cosmetic damage. It's not just like our paint is chipped or our door handles are broken.

I'm talking in terms of our entire purpose. We've neglected the mission Christ gave us to accomplish.

And here's the real clincher: Jesus is returning any day.

What will He think of our neglect?

POWERLESS AGAINST DISUSE

During World War II, the United States produced warships in astounding numbers. Basically, it was a race to see if we could produce them faster than the Axis powers could sink them. We won the race, and after the war, the navy had more ships on its rosters than it could keep in service. Battleships are expensive to build, and that cost is fairly impossible to recover by dismantling the ships. So the navy came up with a solution—a reserve fleet. These ships would be harbored with minimal maintenance so that they could be activated within 120 days should the need arise.

The best known of these fleets is located in Suisun Bay, California, thirty miles northeast of San Francisco. Today, however, you couldn't find a ship in the fleet that could be ready for naval service within 120 days. Properly called the "Reserve Fleet," it's more commonly, and accurately, called the "Mothball Fleet." Once a mighty fleet (as large as a respectable navy in its own right), the ships here are in serious disrepair. Rusted, corroded, and neglected, they are one by one being tugged away to be turned into scrap metal or (as in the case of one fortunate ship, the USS Iowa) made into museums.

Originally numbering over 350 ships, the fleet is down to a mere 10 ships as of this writing. It is scheduled to disappear entirely by 2017, leaving only twenty tons of heavy metal in the bay waters as evidence to the majesty that once was.

What transformed these mighty ships—the heroes of World War II sea battles—into mildewed and corroded skeletons? What disfigured these vessels into worthless relics of years gone by?

The answer in a word: neglect.

The ships that could engage world powers in battle—and win—were powerless against disuse. And so they sit.

Broken.

Rusting.

Out of commission.

They remind me of local churches who have similarly suffered the disgraces of neglect. Thankfully, we do not rely on the flesh, and the moving of the Spirit does not rest. Yet as disciples of Christ, you and I are engaged in a war which we must win. It is a spiritual war, and our commission, delivered by Christ Himself, was spoken with the assurance of the power we need to engage:

> *And Jesus came and spake unto them, saying, All power is given unto me in heaven and in earth. Go ye therefore, and teach all nations, baptizing them in the name of the Father, and of the Son, and of the Holy Ghost: Teaching them to observe all things whatsoever I have commanded you: and, lo, I am with you alway, even unto the end of the world. Amen.*
> —MATTHEW 28:18–20

And yet, *in the midst of the war,* I'm watching Christians and entire churches assign *themselves* to the mothball fleet.

While the battle rages, they neglect the life-or-death orders given by our Commander.

Sure, they *know* the commission; they've just forgotten its central importance. They've set anchor in the bay convinced that they're prepared to serve "if the need arises" or "when the opportunity comes."

My friend, the opportunity has come. The need is here. We live in a post-Christian culture proudly riding a landslide away from the truth. And swept in the landslide are millions—*billions*—of people speeding toward a Christless eternity.

Tragically, while the carnage takes place around us, we sit in the harbor, our mission neglected, bemoaning the fate of the world.

It's not that we're lazy. No, our churches are full of programs and activities. Our lives are busier than our grandparents would have believed possible. But for all our activity, we never leave harbor. Our ministries become more about service than about reaching lost men and women with the gospel of Jesus Christ.

According to the Barna Group, a nationwide research organization, three out of four Christians in the United Sates (74 percent) will share their faith only through "lifestyle evangelism"—unwilling to be a direct, verbal witness to the lost around them.[1] Only 30 percent (less than one-third) said they personally share the plan of salvation with anyone on a regular basis.[2]

We must not let this pattern continue. We must put our vessels back in commission and once again engage in the battle for souls.

Like the ships in Suisun Bay, I see our churches and individual Christians one by one pulling out of the battle. Great churches of the past stand as museums to what once was, while Christians today are losing influence and silencing their own voices in the cause of Christ.

So here we sit. Distracted. Rusting. Waiting our turn to be turned into museums.

But there is a job to be done! Christ commissioned the local church to be His vehicle for reaching the world with the gospel. Now is not the time to release our commission…or even to merely hold our ground. Now is the time to weigh anchor and reengage our vessels.

OWNING OUR BIBLICAL RESPONSIBILITY

To be entrusted with the gospel is a privilege. To fulfill that trust requires that we own it as a responsibility.

You've seen the sixteen-year-old who can't wait to get behind the wheel. He lives for the moment he will get his driver's license; and in his teenage mind, driving Dad's car is the entitlement that rides on the heels of that license. Then, the very day he is awarded that long-dreamed-of license, he totals Dad's car. That young man had a strong sense of entitlement, but a weak sense of responsibility.

When it comes to the Great Commission, we don't have the luxury of entitlement without responsibility. The church is *Christ's* possession—not ours. And the job *He* has given the church is to reach the world with the gospel in our generation.

The Apostle Paul got it. He saw the responsibility and made it his life purpose: "I am debtor both to the Greeks, and to the Barbarians; both to the wise, and to the unwise. So, as much as in me is, I am ready to preach the gospel to you that are at Rome also. For I am not ashamed of the gospel of Christ: for it is the power of God unto salvation to every one that believeth; to the Jew first, and also to the Greek" (Romans 1:14–16).

Too many Christians today have gotten distracted with entitlement and have forgotten responsibility. While we squabble about issues of "liberty," we neglect a world literally dying and going to Hell.

On one hand, there are the Christians who—like a teenage driver who abandons responsibility for the thrill of entitlement—abandon responsibility to reach the world and rejoice in their personal liberty. Their lives are consumed with defending their right to live in "freedom." They will fiercely defend their liberty to drink alcohol, choose their worship style, or simply live life "my way." Galatians 5:13 instructs, "…use not liberty for an occasion to the flesh, but by love serve one another." Surely this serving one another involves sharing the gospel.

On the other hand, there are Christian leaders who are so focused on policing others' liberty that they neglect the Great Commission. They fiercely preach against sin, but they don't reach out to sinners with personal, consistent compassion. They become critical, self-promoting, fruitless leaders who will nearly break their arms to slap themselves on the back for constantly taking the high road of their own definition…while their lives and churches are failing to reach their communities. Yes, we must live holy lives. But Jesus has called us to bear fruit.

Our responsibility is to reach the world with the gospel. We must own our responsibility and personally engage in the Great Commission of Christ.

A PERSONAL COMMISSION

This Great Commission is for the local church—every local church. It is our responsibility to reach the world with the gospel of Christ.

But what makes up the local church? A missions budget? An outreach program?

No, the local church is comprised of people—you and me.

We can't bemoan any longer the ineffectiveness of the church to reach people with the gospel without personally engaging in the commission Jesus gave to us.

I believe that in our minds we tend to paraphrase Jesus' commission by omitting one word—*ye*. Jesus didn't just say, "Go into all the world and preach the gospel." He said, "Go *ye* into all the world and preach the gospel."

What would it take for you to engage personally in the Great Commission? Instruction? Repairs? Motivation? A reminder of the opportunity to make a difference? I pray this book will deliver all of the above. I write to challenge you to engage personally and passionately in the Great Commission of Christ.

This book explores what has pulled us out of commission. Why don't we evangelize as we should? It examines biblical motivations for reengaging our culture with the gospel. And it gives practical suggestions for getting the job done.

Are you ready to move forward? We'll begin in the next chapter by exploring what has been holding us back.

---

1   Barna Group, "Survey Shows How Christians Share Their Faith" (January 31, 2005), https://www.barna.org/barna-update/5-barna-update/186-survey-shows-how-christians-share-their-faith?#. UoEgtKVvdFw.

2   Barna Group, "Survey Shows How Christians Share Their Faith" (June 25, 2001), https://www.barna.org/barna-update/5-barna-update/53-religious-beliefs-vary-widely-by-denomination#. UoEhNqVvdFw.

T W O

WHY WE DON'T EVANGELIZE

What does every man do when his car stops running? He kicks the tire and lifts the hood. (The kicking the tire part is optional. Primarily it is what you do if you don't know anything about mechanics—a frustration relief.)

Regardless of what you know about the engine or the hoses and wires under the hood, you know the problem is there somewhere. (Or at least there is a good chance that it is.) And you know you are going nowhere until you get the problem under the hood fixed.

This chapter is a look under the hood. It's moving beyond the obvious problem that we're not evangelizing as we should and examining *why* we don't do it.

Why don't we evangelize as we should?

Why are Bible-believing churches not effectively reaching our communities with the gospel of Jesus Christ?

We could simply charge our present actions with a fresh tank of zeal, but if the engine itself is in disrepair, zeal won't carry us far. Let's instead lift the hood and examine the engine.

Why don't we evangelize? I suggest nine reasons. We'll explore these more thoroughly throughout this book, but here is an overview:

PRIDE

Most people credit the greatest detriment to evangelism as fear. We don't witness, they say, because we fear what others will think or how they will respond. I agree that fear keeps us from evangelism, but I believe the root of the issue lies deeper.

Why are we afraid? What holds us back from handing out a gospel tract or inviting someone to church? Why do we fear asking people if they know Christ as Saviour? What are we afraid of?

Rejection.

We don't want to be rejected.

There's something in all of us that wants to be liked. And most of us have discovered that telling people they are sinners on their way to Hell and that Jesus is the only way to Heaven isn't the most popular message.

Of course, there is something to be said for being sensitive to the timing and manner in which you share the gospel, but if our first thoughts when the Holy Spirit prompts our hearts to witness is fear of how we're perceived, we will never evangelize as we should. Our self-consciousness will blind us to the eternal realities of Heaven, Hell, and eternity, and our pride will stunt the fruit of compassion in our lives (more on this in Chapter 4).

My friend and mentor, Dr. Curtis Hutson, often said, "The only alternative to soulwinning is disobedience to God." When I become so filled with pride that I'm more concerned with how I'm perceived than I am with the eternal destiny of the person in front of me, I will be disobedient to God's command to witness.

Part of the reason Paul was effective in ministry was that he was willing to suffer personal rejection to preach the gospel. In 1 Corinthians 1:23 he said, "But we preach Christ crucified, unto the Jews a stumblingblock, and unto the Greeks foolishness."

I'll bet people slammed the door in Paul's face. I know they stoned him (Acts 14:19) and beat him (Acts 16:22–23). But Paul knew he was commissioned to preach the gospel, and that command far outweighed both fear and pride on Paul's scale.

PRIORITIES

This barrier to evangelism closely relates to the previous barrier because our priorities most naturally center around ourselves. We do what we enjoy, what is comfortable, and what brings satisfaction. Our priorities are both selfish and temporal—relative to us and to the here and now. It takes a conscious decision and continued growth in spiritual maturity to shift our priorities to the eternal.

Indeed evangelism *is* a priority. Paul understood this and made it the priority of his life: "For though I preach the gospel, I have nothing to glory of: for *necessity is laid upon me;* yea, woe is unto me, if I preach not the gospel!" (1 Corinthians 9:16).

Necessity is laid upon me.

It's like a flooded basement to a homeowner. The necessity of the situation laid upon you changes your plans for the day. You move all the storage items you can so they won't get damaged. You bail water. You call a plumber. Necessity has been laid upon you, and the water in the basement is presently your top priority.

It's like the harvest season to a farmer. He starts early in the morning and works with lights late into the night to harvest crops. Necessity is laid upon him, and if he doesn't harvest while there's time, he will lose his crops.

If we as God's children are to be about the Father's business, we will have to make it our priority. We will have to sense the necessity and live with eternal priorities.

Lack of witnessing is not always the result of a calloused attitude toward souls. Sometimes it's just fifth or sixth on a list we never get around to finishing. Without eternal priorities, we simply won't evangelize as we should. (We'll come back to this in Chapter 6.)

As a Christian, I believe one of my highest priorities in life is giving the gospel to others—regularly, purposefully. As a pastor, I believe one of my highest priorities is to lead the church I pastor in engaging our community with the gospel—regularly, purposefully. I must preach the priorities Jesus preached and call our church family to align their priorities biblically.

In our church, there are people with wide ranges of priorities—everything from bowling leagues to kids' soccer teams to personal and social hobbies of all kinds. I'm glad for our folks to have diversion in their schedules. I'm all for families playing together and encouraging their kids to push themselves and grow. But at some point, we each have to make a choice of what our *priorities* are. What takes precedence when there is a conflict? What do we *make* time for, and what do we simply *enjoy* time for?

It is my responsibility as a pastor to challenge people to set their priorities on the eternal. I believe a large reason many local churches have lost their urgency to witness is that pastors have failed to urge people to witness. We're hesitant to call for people to align their priorities with eternity because we don't want to seem to imply that our own needs or the needs of those we serve are unimportant. Remember, however, what Jesus said to the matter of priorities: "Seek ye first the kingdom of God and his righteousness" (Matthew 6:33). He spoke these words relative to some of the strongest temporal priorities of life—what we will eat and what we will wear.

Pastors, we've got to call people to keep eternal priorities in their lives. We need to challenge them, equip them, and invite them to join us in seeking first the kingdom of God. (We'll revisit this thought in Chapter 12.)

MISUNDERSTANDING WHAT THE GOSPEL IS (AND ISN'T)

While it is vital that we communicate the gospel message with love (more on this in Chapter 15), the gospel itself is not simply a love for our neighbors. It is not social programs, and it is not measured in terms of the world's perception of us. The gospel is the death, burial, and resurrection of Jesus Christ for our sins. (We'll cover this more thoroughly in Chapter 8.)

When we misunderstand what the gospel is, we find ourselves involved in activities that have nothing to do with actually declaring the gospel…and that may in fact harm our message. For instance, I read of one young man who actually went to a gay pride parade to apologize for the church to the gay community. He wrote as follows:

> I spent the day at Chicago's Pride Parade. Some friends and I, with The Marin Foundation, wore shirts with "I'm Sorry" written on it. We had signs that said, "I'm sorry that Christians judge you," "I'm sorry the way churches have treated you," "I used to be a Bible-banging homophobe, sorry." We wanted to be an alternative Christian voice from the protestors that were there speaking hate into megaphones. What I loved most about the day is when people "got it."[1]

Have Christians sometimes behaved disgracefully to the world and to homosexuals? Yes, and we shouldn't. But what concerned me most in this story was that this young man had lost sight of what the gospel is. He said what he most loved about the day was "when people 'got it.'" But what did they "get" anyway? It wasn't the gospel. Simply saying "sorry" and having people respond in gratitude has not conveyed the message of the gospel. In the end, it does nothing to change anyone's eternal destiny.

Loving your neighbors, giving to the poor, maintaining a Christian testimony—all of these are important in spreading of the gospel, but none of these are actually spreading the gospel. If we want to reach the lost with the gospel, we have to actually share the death, burial, and resurrection of Christ for sin.

LACK OF LEADERSHIP

Beyond *preaching* eternal priorities, spiritual leaders must *live* these priorities. I'm talking specifically to myself and to anyone who assists in the leadership of a local church. If we are to lead our churches in evangelism, we must do just that—lead.

People do what people see. If they don't see us working at reaching the lost, attending soulwinning meetings, going out soulwinning, training new Christians in evangelism, they will not have a pattern to follow.

Paul told the church at Philippi, "Those things, which ye have both learned, and received, and heard, and seen in me, do" (Philippians 4:9). He could say this, of course, because he had a Christian lifestyle worth emulating. These Christians saw him reach the lost. They saw him disciple young Christians. They saw him train others to do the same. They saw him live and breathe to preach the gospel.

If we want to see a revival of people being engaged in evangelism, we as church leaders have to lead the way.

PROGRESSIVE MODELS

Another reason I believe we don't evangelize as we should is because of an unbiblical model of evangelism that has arrested our attention and emulation—the "progressive church."

To be sure, definitions vary, and the word *progressive* means different things to different people. I am, of course, for progress! By and large, however, the progressive church in America isn't keen on the confrontational evangelism practiced in the New Testament.

Many progressive pastors do preach the gospel in their services, and I thank God for anyone who is preaching the gospel of Christ; but they're not often out in the community confronting men and women with their need for salvation…like Jesus did with the woman at the well in John 4.

Those who follow a progressive model often poke fun of confrontational types of soulwinning. They say it doesn't work, that it's awkward and outdated. The vast majority of the people in the church I pastor, however, were reached through someone making a one-on-one visit to their home or meeting at a restaurant, talking to them about their soul, and encouraging them to trust Christ as Saviour. Confrontational soulwinning never works if you don't practice it. Those I know who practice it with sensitivity to the Holy Spirit see great fruit.

The progressive model says if we have a "cool" service and the best program in town, people will come in to see what's going on and will be saved. Sometimes this is true, and obviously, I want unsaved guests who come to our services to be saved. But I don't believe it is the sole method of evangelism.

There's no doubt that people should come to Christ in our church services; but the model we see in the New Testament is that people went everywhere preaching the gospel, sharing the good news of salvation through Jesus Christ.

Jesus' disciples did it, and the early church did as well.

And they departed, and went through the towns, preaching the gospel, and healing every where.
—LUKE 9:6

Therefore they that were scattered abroad went every where preaching the word.—ACTS 8:4

I believe this "everywhere spirit" needs to return to biblical Baptist churches as never before. We need a spirit eager and ready to take the gospel to every neighborhood and every corner of our communities.

The stronger the influence of the "progressive model" in our Baptist churches, the more the biblical model of going out publicly and from house to house is diminished. In our church, I want our services to present the gospel clearly and to compel people to come to Christ. But I don't want to lose the passion to go everywhere—including the highways and hedges—to compel people to come to Christ.

CHURCH PROGRAMS

If you're like me and have been married for thirty plus years or if you have lived in the same house for many years, you have amassed a lot of *stuff*. Your storage places are full, and, if you fail to purge, your living spaces get slowly crowded with knickknacks, pictures, furniture—all of it is good alone but too much together.

Churches accumulate stuff too. Stuff in their bulletins, stuff on their calendars, stuff in their programs—stuff that doesn't really relate to the central purposes of the church but somewhere along the line they were good ideas and got sucked into the flow.

At some point, we have to purge our calendars, bulletins, and programs. Like decluttering the home or office, we have to take a good, hard look at what the program of the church involves and what is truly important. Otherwise, it will be the church itself that prohibits the spread of evangelism. Burdened with unnecessary and unfruitful *stuff*, we'll neglect our core mission—reaching the lost, discipling new Christians, and teaching them to do the same.

One reason we accumulate so many programs, events, and activities (and then more activities) is we're under the faulty assumptions that it is our job to entertain and that more is better. It's like we think that the church with the most programs and activities wins. The tragic side effect of these assumptions is that in the midst of our activity, evangelism gets pushed to the side.

If you lead in the local church, I encourage you to evaluate your church programs. Do you have ministries specifically designed to reach the lost? Are these the core ministries of your weekly calendar? Do few participate in these ministries because they're pulled by the other church programs?

It may be that the priorities in the church are out of line. It may be that you need to scale back on some of your activities, much like cleaning out the garage or the basement. Prayerfully review the church's weekly and annual calendar and ask yourself, "What should be cut out? What should be adjusted?" Answering these questions will likely make it more feasible for the church to once again engage purposefully and actively in reaching the lost with the gospel.

Remember, what gets scheduled gets done. It's not enough to *believe* that soulwinning should be the main thing. We must each *make* it the main thing.

DIVISION

Sometimes it's neither priorities nor programs that distract us from witnessing, but just plain problems—personal people issues.

Church division is a serious issue on many levels. God intends Christian relationships to bring joy into our lives. He wants the church to function as a body—each person gladly contributing to the joint goal of glorifying God and fulfilling the Great Commission.

When we live with continually rupturing relationships or divisive factions in the church, our attention will be drawn away from God's purposes for His church.

Part of the solution to these types of problems in the church may actually be adding an emphasis on and providing opportunities for soulwinning. The best prescription for a sick church is a soulwinning diet! When each person develops the mind of Christ to humbly seek the lost, all are drawn together in the same purpose.

Perhaps you've heard the old redneck story about taking coonhounds out hunting. When the hunter gets ready to go out, he loads all his hounds into the back of his pickup truck. Those hounds go at it, growling, snapping, fighting with each other. But when he releases them from the kennel to send them out on their mission of trailing coons, it's a different story. Free from the kennel and set on a coon trail, the dogs work together in happy unity.

I don't believe church members are like hound dogs! But I do believe problems are magnified when we all have our own agendas, and problems are reduced when we are all aligned with a common goal.

In Philippians, Paul challenged us, "Let this mind be in you, which was also in Christ Jesus" (2:5), and later in the epistle, he specifically asked two people in the church, Euodias and Syntyche, to "be of the same mind in the Lord" (4:2). If we are to reach others with the gospel, personal division must go.

PETTINESS

One of the easiest ways for churches and Christians to get sidetracked from sharing the gospel is by becoming issue-orientated. The issues always seem legitimate, but if the central ideology around which a church connects is a particular set of political views, outside church-to-church affiliations, or hobby horse issues, we set ourselves up for major distraction from the Great Commission.

Perhaps one of the most grievous consequences to any church or group of churches that becomes issue-orientated is the fact that they neglect the main issue of reaching souls! I meet men all over America who have a list of issues with other pastors or ministries, yet they are pitifully fruitless in their personal evangelism. Hence, while they criticize others, their own ministries are suffering the lack of the fruit God intended them to bear.

How do we glorify God? It's not by having the best ministry with the strongest position on hot-button issues. It is by bearing fruit that remains. "Herein is my Father glorified, that ye bear much fruit; so shall ye be my disciples" (John 15:8).

Pettiness and division strangle our compassion for the lost and our obedience to Christ. If we are to obey Christ's command, they simply must go.

UNBELIEF

Perhaps the core of all of our soulwinning failures is unbelief—we don't expect God to bring fruit through our efforts. Why cull your church calendar and labor to exercise biblical priorities, why humble yourself or upset the status quo if you don't believe it's going to make a difference anyway?

The truth is, unbelief is always accurate. If we don't believe God will use our witness to lead people to Christ, we won't witness, and God won't use our failure to witness! In our unbelief, we set the perfect stage for our self-fulfilling prophecies to come true.

God can work in any place, through any person, and in whatever method He chooses. But He often chooses to limit where, when, and how He displays His mighty works to a common element: faith. In His earthly ministry, Jesus often made this choice. Matthew 13:58 records, "And he did not many mighty works there because of their unbelief."

Why don't we evangelize? Why don't we see fruit? "And Jesus said unto them, Because of your unbelief: for verily I say unto you, If ye have faith as a grain of mustard seed, ye shall say unto this mountain, Remove hence to yonder place; and it shall remove; and nothing shall be impossible unto you" (Matthew 17:20).

Today, like never before, we need to stir our faith. We need to look at the harvest around us and see it through eyes of faith—ripe and ready to be harvested. We need to remind ourselves that there is still a Heaven and a Hell, there are still people hungry for the truth, and there is still a Holy Spirit who will empower us to win souls to Christ—if we will just open our mouths and witness. (We'll come back to the need for faith in Chapter 10.)

HOW MUCH WILL IT COST?

If you're like me when you take your car to the mechanic, you're as interested in the cost of repairs as you are in the repairs themselves. The first question on your mind is, "How much will it cost me?" Often, we weigh the cost against the necessity of the repair. A broken CD player may not be worth the cost to fix it, while a broken alternator is.

We've covered nine hindrances to our witness in this chapter: pride, priorities, misunderstanding the gospel, lack of leadership, progressive models, church programs, division, pettiness, and unbelief. These are not broken CD player issues; they're engine issues. Whatever the cost to repair them, it is worth it.

And make no mistake, there is cost involved. Diagnosing the problem doesn't fix it; it simply gives us a direction to work. Mobilizing ourselves back to full engagement in the

Great Commission isn't going to be easy. The cost will involve repentance, faith, risks, prayer, reordered priorities, and time.

Another consideration we might make when weighing the cost of repairs is the value of the vehicle itself. I've had vehicles that weren't worth engine repairs. When the engine gave out, it was time to junk the car.

Remember, however, when we consider the cost of these repairs, we're not talking about the old jalopy that's been parked out on the back forty since it was towed there thirty years ago. We're talking about the local church—God's vehicle of choice for delivering the gospel to the world, the church that Jesus purchased with His own blood.

Yes, there will be cost involved in reengaging the local church in the Great Commission, but is the cost worth it? Absolutely!

What is the bottom line—what is the actual cost going to be? We will explore this cost and the solutions to our problems in the coming chapters.

---

1   J. Paul Nyquist and Carson Nyquist quoting Nathan Albert in *The Post-Church Christian: Dealing with the Generational Baggage of Our Faith* (Moody Publishers, 2013), 38.

PART TWO

ENGAGING AS SOULWINNERS

THREE

THE HEART OF
A SOULWINNER

My first recollection of public soulwinning was at Hellyer Park in San Jose, California. I was in seventh grade and eager to share my faith. For some reason, this large park and the shopping mall nearby were the areas where we as teenagers first learned to speak to people about Jesus Christ. Although our presentation wasn't especially polished, we shared the gospel with many people. In that sharing, an aspiration for eternal motives was established in my heart.

The people I admired most were soulwinners. My mom had taken me out soulwinning and made visits to kids who rode her church bus route every week since I was eight years old. I was privileged to grow up in a church where the leadership of the church were active soulwinners. Looking back, I can see there was a neglect of passionate follow up and discipleship. However, adding discipleship to our emphasis, it has been my priority to maintain that zeal for souls that was instilled in my heart in those early days.

I've tried to be a faithful witness now for over four decades. Over the years, I've come to understand that it's not just the act of "going out soulwinning" that makes an effective witness. It's the condition of the heart compelled by the love of Christ that makes a truly great soulwinner. When a pure-hearted Christian witnesses in the power of the Spirit, great things happen to the glory of God.

WHAT IS A SOULWINNER?

The term *soulwinner* is often shunned and sometimes ridiculed by the modern church. Some people misunderstand the term because they believe it implies the "soulwinner" does the work of conversion—like when a young Christian points to someone and says, "He saved me." Of course, the soulwinner didn't *save* the new Christian; he merely told him how he could be saved.

I like the word *soulwinning*, however, because it is a derivative of Bible words. Proverbs 11:30 tells us, "He that winneth souls is wise." Proverbs 14:25 further says, "A true witness delivereth souls: but a deceitful witness speaketh lies." From these verses, we derive the terms *soulwinning* and *soulwinner*. In a very real sense, you and I aren't so much the "soulwinner" as we are the "witness." The true soulwinner is the Holy Spirit. He does the delicate work of conversion (John 16:7–9), but we are His mouthpieces. Like the witness who delivers souls in Proverbs 14:25, we are soulwinners as we speak the truth of the gospel so others may respond to the work of the Holy Spirit in regeneration.

THE ENGINE OF OUR ACTIONS

Pretend for a moment that you've just looked out your front window. You can hardly believe it, but parked in front of your house is a shiny new vehicle. It's this year's model, in your choice of color, with a new car scent you can smell from the house. You turn around, and your spouse is standing behind you dangling a key. The vehicle is yours.

You race outside and open the driver's door. It has every gadget you could imagine—heated seats, individual DVD players for each rider, a built-in GPS…everything.

You excitedly slide into the driver's seat, and your spouse jumps into the passenger seat. Your hand trembles as you place the key into the ignition. You still can't believe this car is actually *yours*.

You turn the key, prepared for the engine to roar to life. Only…it doesn't.

Nothing—not even a click.

You pull the key out, reinsert it, and turn it again.

Nothing.

At that moment, your spouse speaks up and says, "Actually, Honey, it doesn't have an engine. It was cheaper that way."

When it comes to our witness, I'm afraid many of us have gone the cheap route—doing the work of God without having the power of the Holy Spirit working in our lives. We do the work, put in the time—but we have no real heart for God within. We're good at going through motions and creating programs, but too often we neglect what should be the starting place—our hearts. In a later chapter, we will learn the importance of being controlled and directed by the Holy Spirit, but that will never happen unless our hearts are passionate for God, seeking Him first and fully.

Spiritual fruitfulness doesn't begin with frenzied activity. It begins with a real heart for God—a heart fervently in love with and fully surrendered to Jesus.

As we will see in a moment, a Christian with a heart for God will witness for Him. But a Christian who witnesses without first having a heart for God and maintaining a love for Him will, at best, have a shallow witness void of lasting spiritual fruit.

As I read the biographies of great men and women of the faith, people such as Hudson Taylor, Adoniram Judson, D.L. Moody, Mary Slessor, Amy Carmichael, Charles Spurgeon, and R.A. Torrey, I'm always struck by two facts about their lives. First, I'm impressed by the depth of their love for the Lord. When you read their personal letters and journals, it's convicting how deeply they loved Christ and how that love motivated their service.

Second, I'm struck by the fact that these men and women were personal soulwinners. Although they are often remembered for the larger picture of leading ministries or preaching to great audiences, in their day-to-day lives, they were personal soulwinners with tremendous effectiveness for the Lord. And I believe, without a doubt, that their fruitfulness for Christ was directly connected to their hearts for Him.

These men and women had hearts to make Christ known, but it was because they first knew Him in an intimate, personal, love-driven relationship.

Missionary Hudson Taylor made the connection obvious when he wrote, "With *God* all things are possible, and no conviction ever takes place save by the almighty power of the *Holy Ghost*. The great need, therefore, of every Christian worker is to know *God*" (emphasis original).[1]

Notice he didn't say, "The great need of every Christian worker is a polished gospel presentation" or "a great course in sharing your faith." He said the greatest need is *to know God.*

This was the great, overwhelming desire of the Apostle Paul's heart. Paul—arguably the greatest soulwinner of the first century—expressed the deep longing of his heart in five simple words: *"That I may know him"* (Philippians 3:10).

Paul had more obvious "soulwinning" desires as well. He felt a deep burden for the lost. In Romans 9:2–3 he said, "I have great heaviness and continual sorrow in my heart. For I could wish that myself were accursed from Christ for my brethren, my kinsmen according to the flesh."

Yet, Paul's heart for the lost was based on his heart for God. It was the *fruit* of his walk with God, not the *root*. If you and I are going to bear fruit that remains, we must be firmly rooted in a real walk with God. That must be the engine of anything we do for Him.

BEINGS BEFORE DOINGS

Consider a husband who weekly gives two hours toward his wife's to-do list. He makes household repairs, cuts the grass, and washes the car. You would likely say he is a good husband.

But what if this same man ignored his wife the rest of the week? What if he never spoke a word to her, never listened to what she said to him, but simply put in his two hours of service each week out of a sense of duty? Would you still think he is a good husband?

I'm afraid that too often we approach our witness for Christ like this husband approaches his to-do list. We see it as a singular duty and put in weekly hours, but we fail to nurture an ongoing relationship with Jesus and an ongoing sensitivity to the Holy Spirit who wants to empower our witness at other times than just Saturday mornings at 10:00. Without an ongoing relationship with the Lord, eventually, our witness falls away altogether.

We must remember that God created us as human *beings*, not as human *doings*. If we focus on *being* someone with a relationship with God, *doing* things for Him will be the outflow. We are not machines; thus, we must give God our hearts before our actions.

There are many unbiblical ministry models, but one that places an emphasis on what you do for God before who you are before Him is the worst. It leads to fleshly zeal with apparent success, but it leaves the workers full of self and spiritually void of fruit that remains.

Perhaps you, like me, have seen wildly successful soulwinners who were later exposed for having been involved in awful sin—even during their seeming success. They had apparent fruit (and perhaps some genuine conversions in spite of themselves), but there was no root of a genuine walk with God in their hearts.

According to John 15, our fruit-bearing for Christ is directly related to our relationships with Christ.

> *Abide in me, and I in you. As the branch cannot bear fruit of itself, except it abide in the vine; no more can ye, except ye abide in me. I am the vine, ye are the branches: He that abideth in me, and I in him, the same bringeth forth much fruit: for without me ye can do nothing.*
> —JOHN 15:4–5

If we will be Christians who bear fruit for the glory of God, if we will have a lifetime of faithfulness to the Great Commission, we must begin with a sincere, true walk with God in our own lives.

FOLLOW FIRST

When Christ called His disciples, He told them He would make them "fishers of men." Churches who are dedicated to the Great Commission have often picked up on that phrase, encouraging Christians to become fishers of men.

I want you to notice, however, that being a fisher of men is the result of first following Christ. Jesus said, *"Follow me,* and I will make you fishers of men" (Matthew 4:19).

We must get the order right. Our first call is to follow, and the evidence of that will be that He will make us fishers of men.

Mark 3:14 records a similar order: "And he ordained twelve, that they should be with him, and that he might send them forth to preach." He first ordained them to be with Him and then to preach of Him.

Both aspects are important: following and fishing, time with Him and preaching. But the order of both is also important. If we attempt to fish for men and preach the gospel without following the Lord personally and spending time with Him, we won't have His power in our witness.

Simply put, our walk with God—or the lack of it—has a direct effect on our witness.

A THERMOMETER FOR OUR LOVE

The truth that we must first nurture hearts for God before we witness of Him in no way downplays the importance of our witness. It actually strengthens it—but for the right reasons.

If I don't witness, it is an indication that I don't love the Lord as I should. Jesus plainly said, "If ye love me, keep my commandments" (John 14:15). And His last commandment was, "Go ye into all the world, and preach the gospel to every creature" (Mark 16:15). Thus, if I'm not sharing the gospel, it is evidence that my love for Christ has waned.

MOTIVES MATTER

When we look at our hearts before we look at our witness, we are forced to examine our motives. I've heard well-meaning preachers teach that motives in Christian work don't matter. Whether you are driven of duty or impassioned by love makes no difference. Their reasoning is that if you present the gospel and someone trusts Christ, the person is saved regardless of the motive behind your witness.

There is an element of truth to this argument. If I'm trapped in a burning house and you rescue me, it makes no difference to me if you did it because you loved me or because you wanted your picture on the front page of the newspaper as a hero. Either way, I'm rescued. Similarly, when people share the gospel with impure motives, souls may still be saved, and that's a wonderful result.

Paul wrote of this in Philippians 1:15–18: "Some indeed preach Christ even of envy and strife; and some also of good will: The one preach Christ of contention, not sincerely, supposing to add affliction to my bonds: But the other of love, knowing that I am set for the defence of the gospel. What then? notwithstanding, every way, whether in pretence, or in truth, Christ is preached; and I therein do rejoice, yea, and will rejoice."

But there's another side to motives. To say that the end result is *all* that matters is to discount *God's* emphasis on the heart. In the Sermon on the Mount, Christ said, "Blessed are the pure in heart: for they shall see God" (Matthew 5:8). The purity of our motives may make no difference to the person to whom we witness, but it *does* make a difference to God. (And I believe it makes a difference in the ultimate depth and length of our ministry for God.)

There are many motivators to win souls. We could be compelled by the reality of Hell, the desire to make a difference, the example of others, or a sense of duty to Christ's command. All of these are legitimate motives, but they are not enough.

The *constraining* motivation—the motive that propels us from our comfort zone into real witness for God—is the love of Christ. "For the love of Christ constraineth us; because we thus judge, that if one died for all, then were all dead" (2 Corinthians 5:14).

If it is the love of Christ that constrains us, this brings us back to the need to know His love.

Do you have a personal walk with God? Do you spend time in His Word on a regular basis? Do you have an active intercessory prayer life? Has the love of Christ so gripped your heart that you have no choice but to wholly live and personally witness for Him?

WHO MATTERS MOST

One reason we address the engine of having a heart for God before we look at the mechanics of our witness is the tendency to be prideful and contentious amongst ourselves. While claiming to do the work of God, we so easily undermine the very work we have been called to perform.

Consider the ministry of John the Baptist—the man handpicked by God before his birth to prepare hearts for Christ. John had a marvelous ministry. He preached, and great numbers of people responded.

But what made John's ministry so great? It wasn't his ability to blend with the culture. His camel-hair girdle and locust diet were expressions of the fact that he was more in touch with God than he was with culture. It wasn't his smooth speech or polished message. He had neither.

John's ministry was blessed of God because of his heart for God and his humility before God. It was John who said of Christ, "He must increase but I must decrease" (John 3:30). To John, it was all about Jesus—not about himself.

Too often, we make our soulwinning about *us* instead of about *Christ*. We witness because we want to be "good Christians" or alleviate the guilt of not sharing our faith. And our pride manifests itself in our quickness to inspect the work of others. We're constantly evaluating and comparing to others. We spend our time critiquing and criticizing rather than evangelizing and edifying.

We are all susceptible to the clutches of pride. We're all human, so we naturally tend to make ourselves the center of what we do—yes, even of what we do "for God."

If we are to reengage fully in the Great Commission, if we who serve in local churches are to see a soulwinning revival, we will have to start with our hearts. We must ask God to search and cleanse our motives, we must seek Him first and fully, and we must witness to serve Him rather than to impress others or ourselves.

Let pride wars be over. This isn't about us—it's about Him!

START HERE...AND GO FURTHER

All genuine ministry and lasting fruit begins with a heart for God and surrender to the Holy Spirit. Do you want to reach people with the gospel of Christ? Do you want to invest your life as a laborer in His harvest? Start here—with your heart for God.

But here's the thing—and an important thing—it doesn't end here. A heart for God is the engine of ministry. Let that heart compel you to see the world as God does and to witness to others of Christ's salvation.

And then, go *ye*.

---

1   J. Hudson Taylor, *A Retrospect* (China Inland Mission, n.d.), 35.

FOUR

THE CONVICTIONS
OF A SOULWINNER

I'll never forget our tour guide at the Temple of Heaven in Beijing, China. She was knowledgeable, kind, and clearly proud of China's rich heritage.

Her English was a bit broken but better, I'm sure, than my Chinese would sound, even if I'd studied it for several years. And when I broached the subject of eternity to her, she was happy to dialog in English.

I carefully explained the gospel to her, and she listened intently. As I spoke of Christ's death, burial, and resurrection, I could tell she was tracking the story, even through the language barrier. But as I concluded the gospel, explaining Christ's free offer of salvation, she asked a question I will never forget: "Do you really believe that?"

To her atheistically programmed mind, the gospel was incredible—unbelievable. To have an educated American explaining what seemed like a make-believe story intrigued and perplexed her. What God would come and die for His creation's sins? And what educated American would believe this fairy tale?

This dear lady did not trust Christ that afternoon, but I've thought of her question a thousand times since: "Do you really believe that?"

I've thought, too, of another question she asked: "How do you worship your God?" Understandably, she felt that true belief in a higher being must manifest itself in some external actions.

Looking at our calendars, priorities, and the little time we put into sharing the gospel with others, I'm not sure we are in a good position to answer either of her questions.

Do you really believe the gospel? Real belief isn't evidenced by what we *say;* it is evidenced by what we *do.* If we are gripped by the reality of truth, it will change our behaviors.

Do you worship God? We are called to come and worship Christ, then we are commanded to extend that worship through a life of service. In this chapter, we look at the underlying beliefs that accompany obedient witness and service.

WHY CONVICTIONS MATTER

History tells us that strong convictions precede great actions. When a person deeply believes something is true and that it makes a difference, he or she will act on it—for good or bad.

Think, for instance, of William Wilberforce (1759–1833) during the English battle against slavery. He had everything to gain by remaining silent and everything to lose by hanging his career as a politician on an unpopular issue. He spoke up, however, because of his deep conviction that human trafficking is wrong.

The heroes of biblical history also demonstrate this principle. We see Abraham's strong conviction of faith preceding his great action of following God to a land he didn't know. We read of Esther's strong conviction of her responsibility to use her position to save her people preceding her great action of risking her life to deliver her people from death. There are the disciples, whose strong conviction that Christ commanded them to deliver the gospel preceded their great actions of preaching the gospel in spite of persecution. All the way through, God's Word demonstrates the truth that what we believe prompts and stirs our actions.

A love for Christ compels our witness, but biblical convictions propel our witness. If strong convictions precede great actions, what are the biblical convictions of a soulwinner that lead to great actions?

REALITIES AROUND US

As I write, Typhoon Haiyan has recently ravaged the Philippines, leaving heartrending devastation in its wake. Sustained 195 mile per hour winds, with gusts up to 235 miles per hour, and surges of water rising 40 to 50 feet swept away millions of homes and stole thousands of lives. The current death toll is over six thousand, and even that is expected to rise.

Missionaries our church supports have reported tremendous loss, including the deaths of dear Filipino Christians and two Filipino pastors, both graduates of Missionary Rick Martin's Bible college in Iloilo.

What do we do when we hear of the devastating realities others are facing? We rally and give! The Red Cross raised over $16 million and organized volunteer relief efforts throughout the islands.[1] Following the news of the typhoon and how it had devastated brothers and sisters in Christ, our church congregation sacrificially gave thousands of dollars.

There's something about tragedy that evokes immediate response. The pictures, television footage, and YouTube videos all visualize for us the reality of the pain others are enduring, and that realization calls forth a response.

But there are other realities—just as real and tragic—that we neglect. We easily become calloused to the eternal realities around us. There are no heartrending pictures of a lost soul. We have no video footage of Heaven, Hell, or the soul that lives inside of every person we encounter.

But the realities of eternity are no less real. They are no less important. They are just forgotten.

Those of us who know, believe, and desire to share the gospel must make these eternal realities our personal convictions. Convictions are the spark plugs that keep the engine of faith going forward. And biblical convictions regarding the eternal souls of men and women move us forward in reaching the lost for Christ.

HELL

To be frank, I don't like to think about Hell. Who would?

But I don't like to think of the suffering happening in the Philippines right now either. I can block the pain of those in the Philippines from my mind, but it doesn't change their pain. My disregard for the loss caused by Haiyan doesn't bring moms and dads back from the grave. It doesn't release the rows of dead bodies along the streets of Tacloban. It doesn't bring pastors who were killed back to their congregations. It doesn't rebuild houses or churches. It doesn't undo the destruction that has been done. And it certainly doesn't prompt me to give to relieve the suffering. It only makes me feel better.

In the same way, I can block the reality of Hell from my mind. But it doesn't change the facts that there is still a real place called Hell and that the people I talk with will go there if they do not trust Christ as Saviour.

Jesus kept the reality of Hell before His eyes, and He spoke of it often. Perhaps the most known reference is of the rich man and Lazarus in Luke 16:

> And it came to pass, that the beggar died, and was carried by the angels into Abraham's bosom: the rich man also died, and was buried; And in hell he lift up his eyes, being in torments, and seeth Abraham afar off, and Lazarus in his bosom. And he cried and said, Father Abraham, have mercy on me, and send Lazarus, that he may dip the tip of his finger in water, and cool my tongue; for I am tormented in this flame.
> —LUKE 16:22–24

In this passage, Christ details the torment and anguish of Hell. He tells us in other passages of the separation and darkness and of the loss of comfort and light.

> But the children of the Kingdom shall be cast into outer darkness: There shall be weeping and gnashing of teeth.—MATTHEW 8:12

And shall cast them into the furnace of fire: there shall be wailing and gnashing of teeth.—Matthew 13:50

And death and hell were cast into the lake of fire. This is the second death. And whosoever was not found written in the book of life was cast into the lake of fire.—Revelation 20:14–15

If we could view Hell for five minutes, we would never view soulwinning as optional.

Hell is real, and remembering its reality is one of the basic convictions of the gospel that will propel our witness.

THE ETERNAL SOUL

If we believe the Bible, then we believe that every person is born with an eternal soul that will live somewhere forever. Scripture plainly states that those who do not trust Christ as Saviour will spend eternity in Hell,[2] and those who receive Christ's gift of salvation will spend eternity in Heaven.[3]

These are weighty convictions. And they must compel great action on our part. We must warn people of their lost condition and point them to Christ.

ONE WAY OF SALVATION

The salvation offered through Jesus Christ is as real as eternity and Hell. Although the world increasingly disdains the exclusive claims of the gospel, Acts 4:12 declares that salvation is available *only* through Jesus: "Neither is there salvation in any other:

for there is none other name under heaven given among men, whereby we must be saved."

I remember an encounter that took place when I was a teenager. I was in the parking lot at Eastridge Mall in San Jose, California, and I handed a lady a gospel tract. I invited her to one of our church services and asked if I could ask her one further question.

"Go right ahead," she encouraged.

"Ma'am, do you know if you were to die, whether you would spend eternity in Heaven or Hell, or don't you know?"

Ready to enlighten me, she responded, "Son, Heaven is a lot like this mall. There are many roads that lead to the mall, and any one of them is good. In the same way, there are a lot of different religions, but they will all lead to the same place. And they are all good."

If you know and believe the Bible, you immediately realize the grave fallacy of this all-too-prevalent philosophy. Jesus plainly said, "I am the way, the truth, and the life: no man cometh unto the Father, but by me" (John 14:6).

You and I believe John 14:6, but I'm concerned that we've forgotten the reality of Jesus' words. We give lip service to the truth that salvation is exclusively available through Christ, but we live as if everyone around us is okay. We don't make the effort to share the truth of salvation with people who are on a real road to a real Hell.

If all religious roads lead to the same place, why would I witness to anyone? The simple answer is that I wouldn't. Similarly, if I forget that others around me are most likely on the broad road to destruction (Matthew 7:13), why would I make an effort to warn them of coming destruction? The simple answer is that I wouldn't.

A *Newsweek* religion survey reported that many evangelical Christians have lost their bearings on eternal realities. Surveyors asked people who professed to be born-again Christians, "Can a good person who does not share your religious beliefs attain salvation or go to Heaven?" An unbelievable 68 percent answered "yes."[4]

When Jesus spoke with Nicodemus, He was straightforward and told the religious leader, "Ye *must* be born again" (John 3:7). Christ lived with an awareness of the realities of eternity, and because of that, He gave a faithful witness to others.

We know these basic gospel convictions—that every person has an eternal soul, that Hell is real, and that Heaven is freely offered. But let me ask you the question my Chinese guide asked me: "Do you really believe that?" If we really believe and remember these truths concerning eternity and salvation, we will be passionate to tell others of Christ. These convictions will carry us out to the harvest field.

HEAD TO HEART

Remember algebra class in high school when you learned theoretic concepts, but they never really gripped your heart? Too often, this is how we treat the convictions of the gospel. Theologically we know them to be true, but practically we forget they are as real as the person standing in front of us at the grocery checkout or the person who delivers our paper each morning. Somehow these truths never move from our heads to our hearts.

Christ's heart overflowed with compassion. Five times in the gospels we read that Jesus was "moved with compassion,"[5] and six additional times we see direct reference to the compassion of Christ.[6] Jesus felt the needs of others. He kept eternal realities before His eyes, and they influenced His actions.

Compassion grounded in a conviction of eternal realities moves us to action so much so that we can gauge our compassion by our action.

A Christian with the heart of Christ will express compassionate belief in the realities of eternity in at least two ways.

First, he or she will have the compassion to pray. When we think of compassion we usually think more in terms of rushing to help. But one of the most compassionate acts we can do is pray. In fact, this is what Jesus actually told us to do when His heart was moved with compassion.

> But when he saw the multitudes, he was moved with compassion on them, because they fainted, and were scattered abroad, as sheep having no shepherd. Then saith he unto his disciples, The harvest truly is plenteous, but the labourers are few; Pray ye therefore the Lord of the harvest, that he will send forth labourers into his harvest.—MATTHEW 9:36–38

This is the only prayer request Jesus ever gave us. He saw the reality that the multitudes were like sheep without a shepherd. He expressed the conviction that the harvest is plenteous but there are not enough laborers. He then asked us to pray that God would send more laborers into the harvest.

Has this prayer request made it to your prayer list? Are you asking the Lord to raise up soulwinners with a heart of compassion for the lost?

One benefit of praying for this need is that it reminds you of the reality that the harvest needs more laborers. It motivates you to labor in the harvest fields yourself. It's difficult to pray very long for dedicated soulwinners without being diligent in your own soulwinning.

The other way we will express compassion is by following through and doing something to make a difference. While the Gospel of Matthew tells us that Jesus was moved with compassion to *pray,* the synoptic account in the Gospel of Mark tells us that He was moved with compassion to *teach.*

> *And Jesus, when he came out, saw much people, and was moved with compassion toward them, because they were as sheep not having a shepherd: and he began to teach them many things.*—MARK 6:34

The compassion of the Lord moved Him to see the need and take the lead. When we see people through the eyes of compassion, when gospel convictions move from our heads to our hearts, we will take action.

Some people are seized with short bursts of compassion, thus they have only short bursts of responding action. Their compassion is based on emotion, rather than convictions of eternal realities. If we want to make a difference for the long haul, however, and if we want to continually respond to the convictions of the gospel, we'll have to work this action into our regular routines. Soulwinning is not an activity to fit in as it works or an opportunity to take advantage of if it happens across your path. It is a divine commission from Christ, and it is a priority to purposefully schedule into your life.

Without a doubt, there are people where you live and with whom you interact who do not know Christ. And without a doubt, there are people around you who would trust Christ if you told them the good news of the gospel.

The question is: will you?

HEAVENLY AFFECTIONS

The greater our sense of eternal realities, the greater will be our desire to make an eternal difference. Colossians 3:1–2 challenges us, "If ye then be risen with Christ, seek those things which are above, where Christ sitteth on the right hand of God. Set your affection on things above, not on things on the earth."

The average, fleshly-minded American Christian wants their "best life now." They want to please and enjoy themselves. They want to be great. They want to achieve personal goals. They want inspiration and motivation for this life.

Christ did promise to give "life…more abundantly" (John 10:10). He provides joy and satisfaction, right now, in this life. But He didn't come to give us our "best life now." He came to make us ready for the life that is to come. And when we have deep-seated convictions about the realities of the life that is to come, we will invest our energies there.

In recent years, especially since I crossed my fiftieth birthday, I've noticed that as men who passionately love the Lord grow older, they also grow more focused in their desire to live for eternity. It's as if the more they mature as a Christian, the more they recognize the futility of investing their lives in anything except eternity. Their convictions deepen with growth in the Lord, thus their actions reflect these strong convictions.

I don't know if angels ever yawn, but if they do, I would imagine they do it during most of our moments of greatest excitement—when our favorite team scores a touchdown, when we drive a hole-in-one, when our hunting bullet successfully finds its mark in big game, or when our favorite meal is set in front of us.

It's not that angels are calloused. It's just that they have something so much greater to rejoice in: "Likewise, I say unto you, there is joy in the presence of the angels of God over one sinner that repenteth" (Luke 15:10).

I'm thankful for the many pleasures the Lord gives us, including sports, hunting, and good meals. But I want to find my greatest joy in what initiates the cheers of Heaven—the salvation of a lost soul. And I want to focus my energy in leading that soul to Christ!

I want my heart to reflect the heart of the Good Shepherd who will "go after that which is lost, until he find it...And when he hath found it, he layeth it on his shoulders, rejoicing" (Luke 15:4–5).

Why is it that we make much of that which has no eternal significance while neglecting that which matters most in eternity? Perhaps it is because we have allowed our convictions concerning Heaven, Hell, and eternal salvation to dull.

We so easily become sidetracked from the task Christ has given us, and without knowing it, our hearts become cold—deadened to the convictions of the soulwinner.

DO YOU REALLY BELIEVE THAT?

We've looked at basic gospel convictions and the compassion behind them that should motivate us to witness. Let's go back to my Chinese guide's question: *Do you really believe that?*

I'm venturing to guess that you do. But what if you believe it but don't feel compassion to respond? What do you do then?

I suggest five responses to these convictions:

1. Develop compassion through reading Scripture. If you have to read about the rich man in Hell or Christ's crucifixion every morning to remember the realities of eternity and the suffering Christ endured to save people, do it! Read also through the gospels, and notice Christ's compassion—and His resulting actions.

2. Pray—for compassion and for people. It's so easy for the realities of eternity to get swallowed up in the realities of our busy schedules. Don't allow your burden for people to get buried in projects, meetings, and memos. The only way I know to sustain a heartfelt burden for souls is to pray daily for God to help me see lost people with His compassion. If this is not on your prayer list, it probably won't remain on your schedule.

3. Act on every impulse of the Holy Spirit. Any Christian who has grown at all has felt the prompting of God's Spirit to witness to someone. And that prompting is probably accompanied by a sense of the reality of eternity. But too often we silence these prompts because we are either too busy or too uncomfortable (i.e., proud) to obey. Develop a habit of responding to the impulses of the Holy Spirit to witness, and I promise you, you will develop compassion at the same time.

4. Make sacrifices. When our church gave so generously to the needs in the Philippines after Haiyan struck, it was right after a generous offering at the close of our annual missions conference. Because our church had just given so generously after missions conference, I know this second offering represented sacrifice.

The sacrifices you make for soulwinning may be in your schedule. They may be in your finances. They may be in ways that no one else will ever know. But they must be somewhere. If you really believe in something—such as the convictions of the gospel and the realities of eternity—you will sacrifice for it. And sacrificing for it will increase your sense of its importance.

5. Go soulwinning. Time and again I have found that the best way to stir my compassion for the lost is to take time to share the gospel. If I wait for the feelings of compassion to come, they rarely do. But if I do the actions of compassion based on conviction rather than feeling, the feelings of compassion return.

You and I know the gospel. The question is, do we really believe that? There is one way to prove that we do—tell someone about Christ.

1   American Red Cross, "Red Cross Increases Support to Typhoon Haiyan to $16 Million" (November 27, 2013), http://www.redcross.org/videos/Red-Cross-Increases-Support-to-Typhoon-Haiyan-to-16-Million.

2   Revelation 20:15.

3   1 Peter 1:3–5.

4   Jerry Adler, "In Search of the Spiritual" (Newsweek, September 5, 2005), 48–49.

5   Matthew 9:36; 14:14; 18:27; Mark 1:41; 6:34.

6   Matthew 15:32; 20:34; Mark 5:19; 8:2; Luke 7:13; 10:33.

FIVE

THE PASSION
OF A SOULWINNER

His name was common, but his prayers were not. John Smith, a nineteenth-century English circuit-riding preacher, was called "the man with calloused knees." For hours at a time, he would pour out his supplications to the Lord.

I'm sure Smith had personal needs for which he prayed. I'm sure he prayed for his family, friends, and the people he ministered to in the churches of his circuit. But the continual prayer of his heart for which he is famous was none of those. It was a simple sentence packed with unbelievable passion: "God, give me souls or else I die."

YOUR HEART'S DESIRE

When was the last time you wanted something so badly you thought you'd die without it? Perhaps it was something you once had—a relationship or a position. Once it was stripped from you, you thought you couldn't live without it, and regaining it became the passion of your heart.

Perhaps it was something you did not yet have—and every thought of your life revolved around earning it.

The passion of a fruitful soulwinner's heart is no less intense than the greatest passion you've ever known. It's simply focused in a different direction—toward souls.

I'll never forget June 6, 1986, when Terrie and I and our two young children came to Lancaster, California. We drove our blue Mitsubishi station wagon followed by a Ryder truck, and moved into a tiny duplex on Spearman Avenue.

The church that had called me as their pastor had fewer than twenty people attending and a negative balance in the bank. Our diet consisted mostly of Ramen noodles and peanut butter sandwiches.

When we came to Lancaster, there was one overwhelming desire in our hearts—to see souls saved.

Many evenings, I'd drive that blue Mitsubishi out to Vista Point—a lookout over our Antelope Valley—and observe the thousands of lights below. I'd consider the people those lights represented and earnestly pray for their salvation.

These days, when I feel I've become too focused on administration or too concerned with the opinions of critics, I go back to that vista and ask God to reset my priorities for the souls of men.

God places this passion—to see others saved—in our hearts at salvation.

The Apostle Paul clearly had it. In Romans 1:13 he summarized his whole desire to go to Rome: "Now I would not have you ignorant, brethren, that oftentimes I purposed to come unto you, (but was let hitherto,) that I might have some fruit among you also, even as among other Gentiles." Paul didn't want to go to Rome to experience the fine culture or to see the renowned architecture. He wanted fruit in Rome.

Perhaps you remember the immediate burden you sensed after your salvation for those you loved who didn't know Christ. And perhaps, like so many of us, you've also sensed that passion wane.

I know by experience that it's easy to lose it. Slowly, usually imperceptibly were it not for the Holy Spirit's conviction, the passion ebbs from our hearts and is replaced with our own selfish passions. Our eyes lose their focus on eternity, and we shift our gaze to the here and now and invest our energies in building comfortable lives for ourselves.

If we are going to obey Christ's commission, our passion must be His passion. Our hearts' desire must match His heart's desire.

THE PASSION OF CHRIST

When Jesus walked in Palestine, He had a singular focus: "For the Son of man is come to seek and to save that which was lost" (Luke 19:10).

Christ's passion was not for better social systems or relief from Roman oppression. It wasn't that every person in Israel be healed. It wasn't fame or influence.

If Jesus had come in the twenty-first century, He could have amassed a large following on Twitter and had a Facebook fan page that broke all records. He could have built a personal platform and set social networks buzzing with His updates. He could have developed great church programs, been the keynote speaker of impressive conferences, written best-selling books, and innovated new ministry strategies. But I don't think He would have—because He didn't do the first-century counterparts.

To be sure, Jesus *did* attract a following. But He didn't focus on the aspects of ministry that tend to consume our attention. For Jesus, life wasn't about managing His image or creating a strong brand. It was about loving people and meeting their deepest spiritual need—salvation.

The passion of Christ was overwhelmingly clear—to seek and to save the lost. His mission was to bring salvation.

In ministry today—in everyday life, for that matter—our passions are easily focused on ourselves. We want recognition and influence, and we have the tools to gain both. With the powers of social media and the Internet, we can now broadcast ourselves to the world like never before—and have people listen. With or without social media, our hearts' desires tend to be self focused and—when held against eternity—shortsighted. Sadly, many widely read Christian bloggers or Internet influencers rarely personally lead others to Christ. They have become known, but they are not making Christ known.

What really matters? Gaining a following or winning souls? Innovating programs or investing ourselves into eternity?

The bringing of one soul to Christ is the highest achievement possible to human life. I bet no one will ever win a Nobel Prize for it; nevertheless, it *is* the highest achievement—and I want to do it again and again. In fact, I want bringing souls to Christ to be my passion and lifelong mission.

HIS PASSION, OUR MISSION

When Christ's ministry was finished, His passion wasn't. All over the world, there were people for whom He had died who had not yet received Him as their Saviour. Most had not so much as even heard they could.

And so Christ gave His disciples clear instructions. We call it the "Great Commission":

> *Go ye therefore, and teach all nations, baptizing them in the name of the Father, and of the Son, and of the Holy Ghost: Teaching them to observe all things whatsoever I have commanded you: and, lo, I am with you alway, even unto the end of the world. Amen.*
> —Matthew 28:19–20

I don't think He could have been more clear. In one sentence, He defined a concise mission.

The eleven men to whom Christ delivered these instructions understood them perfectly, and they set about obeying them. History tells us that they ultimately gave their lives in the performing of Christ's instructions.

But these instructions are ours as well. Christ has *commanded* us to deliver the gospel to the lost, baptize them, and disciple them. If our lives are not wrapped around these instructions, we're living with inferior passions and disobedient actions.

AN IMPASSIONED BURDEN

In the previous chapter, it was clear that when Christ saw the needs of people, He was burdened for them and was moved with compassion. The realities of eternity burdened His soul and motivated His actions.

But Christ's burden didn't stop with Himself. Matthew 9:36 records that Christ saw the multitudes and was moved with compassion on them. The very next verse tells us, "Then saith he unto his disciples…." Because Christ's heart was stirred, He wanted His disciples to share His burden. It is this shared burden among many people that will make soulwinning in a community effective and effectual.

You and I must learn to see people through the eyes of Christ. In our narcissistic society and with our selfish tendencies, this is a challenge indeed. It requires a decision on our part. We'll never just "happen" to gain a burden for the lost. We must choose to see people as Christ saw them. We must make His passion our passion. And we must involve others in doing the same. (We'll come back to how specifically we can do this throughout Part 3 of this book.)

UNSTOPPABLE DETERMINATION

Any mission of consequence will encounter obstacles. For some people, obstacles squelch progress. For others, obstacles strengthen their passion to overcome.

A prime example of passion-fueled determination is seen in the life of the Apostle Paul. It is obvious that Paul was gripped with the passion to obey Christ's command and spread the gospel.

He saw himself as a debtor—under a moral obligation to preach the gospel: "I am debtor both to the Greeks, and to the Barbarians; both to the wise, and to the unwise" (Romans 1:14).

He was tenaciously prepared in his spirit and personally prepared with a message: "So, as much as in me is, I am ready to preach the gospel to you that are at Rome also" (Romans 1:15).

He was persuaded that the realities of eternity trumped every other visible, tangible reality in his life—including pride and persecution: "For I am not ashamed of the gospel of Christ: for it is the power of God unto salvation to every one that believeth; to the Jew first, and also to the Greek" (Romans 1:16).

He was settled in his conviction that all people everywhere must put their trust in Christ: "For therein is the righteousness of God revealed from faith to faith: as it is written, The just shall live by faith" (Romans 1:17).

This is the passion of a soulwinner. It brings an unstoppable determination to overcome all obstacles to reach people for Christ.

When I think of overcoming obstacles, I'm reminded of one our West Coast Baptist College graduates, Nathan Kinoshita, missionary to Tokyo, Japan. When Nathan and his wife, Ruth, went to Tokyo to begin church planting, the city was credited as the most expensive city in the world in which to live. It bumps up and down on the list (as of this writing, it is the sixth most expensive city), but it remains high. The expense not only impacted their personal living needs (for $2,500 per month, they rent a five hundred-square-foot apartment for their family of five), but it impacted their ministry needs as well. To rent even a small building in which to hold services for three hours each Sunday costs them $7,000 per month. On top of that, Japan is not known as a mission field that is particularly responsive to the gospel. So the Kinoshitas were looking at months, possibly years, before a self-supporting church would be established.

Many people would have said, "It can't be done. It's too expensive. There are too many obstacles. The people don't want to hear anyway."

I'm thankful Nathan Kinoshita didn't say that. He found an apartment for his family and rolled up his sleeves and went to work sharing the gospel. Today, a mere five and a half years later, the City Baptist Church of Tokyo is strong, healthy, and growing.

Obstacles are what we see when we take our eyes off the goal. Passion is what we need to overcome the obstacles.

ENEMIES OF SOULWINNING PASSION

Do you know what undermines your passion? What defuses your zeal for the gospel and sabotages your determination to overcome obstacles? There are many obstacles of soulwinning passion, but there are four primary obstacles:

1. Selfishness—It comes in so many shapes and sizes. We rarely think, "I don't want to witness because I care more about myself than others," but our actions speak for themselves. It's all too easy to be so consumed with ourselves—our goals, plans, entertainment, etc.—that we neglect to make time to share the gospel with others. Sometimes selfishness manifests itself when we fail to schedule soulwinning opportunities, and sometimes it manifests itself when we resist the prompting of the Lord to witness during our regular routines because we don't have time.

2. Apathy—Really a form of selfishness, apathy numbs our hearts to the spiritual needs of those around us. It dulls our ability to hear the promptings of the Holy Spirit to witness. And it deadens our willingness to take risks for the sake of the gospel. Apathy is the sad result of a waning love for Christ.

3. Unbelief—The Great Commission will only be accomplished by people who dare to have faith in God. Too many Christians have bought into the lie that their effort in obeying Christ's command wouldn't make a difference anyway.

It's true that I can't do everything. But I can do *something!* As Helen Keller so aptly said, "I am only one, but still I am one. I cannot do everything, but still I can do something; and because I cannot do everything, I will not refuse to do the something that I can do."[1]

4. Misplaced priorities—There is a snowball effect to a lessening of passion. When we become wrapped up in ourselves, we lose compassion for others and tend toward apathy. An apathetic heart is naturally unlikely to surge forward in faith. Soon, this selfish apathy and unbelief colors our decisions and shapes our priorities. Why go soulwinning if it doesn't make a difference anyway? And why choose to believe that it does make a difference when you really don't care that a difference is needed? It's a vicious cycle, and it can only result in disobedience to Christ.

Our priorities—at least as we live them out—define the success or failure of our lives. This subject is so vital to the Great Commission that we will explore it further in our next chapter.

THE SECRET TO REIGNITING THE PASSION

The enemies of passion are not best overcome by focusing on slaying them, but by focusing on doing what they attempt to stall us from doing. In other words, the secret to reigniting passion is not to conquer every shred of selfishness in our lives but to see it for what it is and to do what it attempts to keep us from doing—sharing the gospel.

If we wait to go soulwinning until we feel passionate—until we have defeated selfishness, apathy, unbelief, and misplaced priorities—we'll never go. But if we attack selfishness, apathy, unbelief, and misplaced priorities by sharing the gospel with someone, we ultimately win. And by sharing the gospel, the passion will return.

When our willingness to go soulwinning depends on our feelings of passion, selfishness wins—we're only doing what we feel like doing. But when we allow the Lord to embed the convictions of the gospel deeply in our hearts, when we remain responsive to the Holy Spirit's promptings to witness on the spot, when we intentionally schedule time for this great priority of life, we stir the embers of our cold, hardened hearts, allowing passion to return.

So what do you do if you don't have a passion for souls? What if there is no burden that stirs your heart to share the gospel? You do it anyway. And that doing is like breathing oxygen into the fire of dormant passion.

PASSIONATE COMMITMENT

One of the great soulwinners of history was David Livingstone— missionary explorer in Africa. As an explorer, he was commissioned by Scotland to find a way through the interior of Africa to its west coast. As a missionary, he preached and witnessed everywhere he went.

Beyond personally leading souls to Christ, Livingstone's great goal was to open the interior of Africa for missionaries to bring the gospel. But his great sorrow was that few missionaries followed him. The sickness, discomfort, and risks held them back.

To Livingstone's deep grief, however, the sickness, discomfort, and risks didn't hold slave traders back. Everywhere Livingstone opened new territory, he found the abominable slave trade following him. In their greed, slave traders were willing to risk their lives and sacrifice their comfort to deal in human trafficking deep in the heart of Africa.

As Livingstone observed this tragedy, he penned a piercing question: "Cannot the love of Christ carry the missionary where the slave trade carries the trader?" In a letter to his father, he passionately wrote, "I shall open up a path to the interior or perish."[2]

If you've read so much as a children's biography about Livingstone or an article about nineteenth-century exploration in Africa, you know that Livingstone didn't bound out of bed each morning eager to conquer a new day. Most of the time, Livingstone was burning with fever. He was frequently abandoned by helpers or captured by natives. He had few supplies and was often hungry, sick, and very lonely.

Livingstone's passion wasn't the surface passion that takes immediate, sometimes superfluous action and then moves on to other interests. His passion wasn't a continual eagerness. It was deeper. It was a commitment—a passionate commitment to obey Christ and to see souls saved. It was born of love for Christ—the kind of passionate love you see in a couple who's been married fifty years and one spouse has Alzheimer's but is still loved and cared for. It's the kind of passion that generates action—even when surface feelings are exhausted.

The passion of a soulwinner is more than a feeling—it is belief-driven action. It's a passionate love for Christ that compels us to share the gospel—even when we don't feel like it, even when it's inconvenient, and even when it's difficult.

Do you have this passion? Do you *want* this passion? Let the love of Christ carry you to take the gospel to the lost souls around you—in your neighborhood, your community, your circles of acquaintance. Passion produces action.

HOW'S YOUR PASSION?

Would you take a moment now and do a quick spiritual inventory? What is your greatest passion? What is your heart's desire?

I'm guessing that whatever your answer, you are daily thinking about it and regularly acting on it. If your passion is to launch a business, write a book, earn a promotion, develop a platform of influence, raise a family, grow a ministry, or any number of worthy goals, you think about it often, discipline yourself to do the actions that make progress, and make sacrifices to achieve.

May God make the deepest desire of our hearts be to see souls saved. May we want it so badly that we pray, "God, give me souls else I die!"

In our next chapter, we'll see practical steps to align our priorities with our passion.

———————————

1   Helen Keller, *Quotes by Helen Keller* (QuotationsBook.com), 6.
2   Thomas Hughes, *The Life of David Livingstone* (A. L. Burt Company Publishers, 1902), 81.

SIX

THE PRIORITIES
OF A SOULWINNER

Take a late night drive through a farming community during harvest season, and you're likely to see massive headlights shining across partially harvested fields. Behind the lights are farmers working through the night to harvest their crops.

Harvest season is brief, and the harvest is precious. Thus, farmers will rise early and toil late to bring it in. They have a sense of urgency that is befitting of the value of their crops.

It is this sense of urgency that Jesus labored to instill in His disciples. To Christ, *people* are valuable.

When Jesus saw people who were without salvation, it moved Him. He saw their spiritual need. He saw them as lost sheep without a shepherd, and He reminded His disciples that the timing of reaching these people was critical.

*But when he saw the multitudes, he was moved with compassion on them, because they fainted, and were scattered abroad, as sheep having no shepherd. Then saith he unto his disciples, The harvest truly is plenteous, but the labourers are few; Pray ye therefore the Lord of the harvest, that he will send forth labourers into his harvest.—*MATTHEW 9:36–38

A CONTRAST OF PRIORITIES

One of Christ's evangelism encounters was with a woman whom, in absence of a recorded name, we tag "the woman at the well." This encounter, recorded in John 4, reveals the bold compassion of Christ as He confronted an outcast of society with her need for a Saviour.

But it reveals something else, too—the priorities of Jesus and of His disciples.

Jesus' encounter with the woman appeared to be a chance meeting, although in the mind of God it was planned. It was noon, and Jesus and His disciples needed food. Because Jesus was weary, He waited at the well while the disciples looked for lunch. While He waited, He met a woman.

You know the story—how Jesus lovingly but directly engaged her in a conversation about her soul. He confronted her sin and revealed Himself as the Saviour. In those moments, the lady changed from a battered and religiously defensive outcast to a repentant sinner.

And that's when the disciples returned: "And upon this came his disciples" (John 4:27). You'd think these men would be praising God for what had just happened. You'd think they would be asking Jesus to tell them line by line how the conversation had unfolded so they could practice their evangelism skills.

But no. Their first question (albeit unspoken) was one of prejudice. Why was Jesus speaking with a Samaritan woman? The Bible says they "marvelled that he talked with the woman: yet no man said, What seekest thou? or, Why talkest thou with her?"

Presently, the lady left Jesus to bring the rest of the town to meet Him.

Now was the disciples' chance. They could ask Jesus how they could have a more passionate heart for souls or what is a good lead-in question to get to speak with someone about eternity.

But what did they voice? "Master, eat."

Really?

A woman broken by society and ravaged by sin just trusts Christ and you want to talk about...*lunch?*

It was to these men with these priorities that Jesus said, "My meat is to do the will of him that sent me, and to finish his work."

HOLY URGENCY

To help the disciples understand the urgency of His priorities, Jesus used a metaphor with which they were familiar—harvest.

> *Say not ye, There are yet four months, and then cometh harvest? behold, I say unto you, Lift up your eyes, and*

look on the fields; for they are white already to harvest.
—JOHN 4:35

Jesus told them, "Like the priority of harvest, so is the priority of evangelism."

Just as a productive farmer will sense an urgency that motivates untiring action, so a fruitful Christian will fervently give of himself or herself to gather a harvest of souls.

It's really a matter of priorities, and of holy urgency.

Harvest is brief, and no farmer can afford to miss it. This is no time to sleep on the job. There are people around us who would respond to the gospel if we would only make it our priority to share it with them.

Paul wrote to the church in Corinth, "Awake to righteousness, and sin not; for some have not the knowledge of God: I speak this to your shame" (1 Corinthians 15:34). Where there are people who have not the knowledge of God, that is to our shame. It means we've been neglecting our responsibility. So let me ask you, are there any in *your* community who have not the knowledge of God?

Our chance for evangelism is brief, and we simply can't lose the harvest. It's too precious to waste. If a farmer will turn his life upside down during harvest season, can we not reorder our priorities for Christ's kingdom?

SAYS WHO?

Your children probably sweetly and immediately obey whatever their siblings ask them to do. Mine didn't.

When I was raising my family, if I told my son Larry to tell his brother Matt to pick up his room, Matt would say, "Says who?" If I told Kristine to tell Danielle to help her mom, Danielle would say, "Says who?"

It was always gratifying to the messenger to say, "*Dad* said!" because they knew their message would be acted on.

We don't drop the "Says who?" mindset when we become adults. We just camouflage it better. When we hear the command to witness, we say, "Well, that's your opinion" or "He thinks it's important, but I believe it is more important that I live out my faith from my home." Or...we just ignore the command altogether.

These are the adult versions of "Says who?" It's a not-so-subtle way of expressing, "What? I can't decide what is important to me? Says who?!"

Says Jesus.

And He has the authority to reorder our priorities.

Even as Christ gave the Great Commission, He prefaced it with a reminder of His authority: "And Jesus came and spake unto them, saying, All power is given unto me in heaven and in earth. Go ye therefore..." (Matthew 28:18–19).

But this authority is also an assurance. All power is His— the power to command us to go and the power to make our going prosperous.

One author said it this way:

> The fundamental basis of all Christian missionary enterprise is the universal authority of Jesus Christ, "in heaven and on earth." If the authority of Jesus were circumscribed on earth, if He were but one

of many religious teachers, one of many Jewish prophets, one of many divine incarnations, we would have no mandate to present Him to the nations as the Lord and Savior of the world. If the authority of Jesus were limited in heaven, if He has not decisively overthrown the principalities and powers, we might still proclaim Him to the nations, but we would never be able to "turn them from darkness to light, and from the power of Satan unto God" (Acts 26:18). Only because all authority on earth belongs to Christ dare we go to all nations. And only because all authority in heaven as well is His have we any hope of success.[1]

THE VALUE OF ONE

Every soul is valuable to God. Christ's parable of the lost sheep in Luke 15 illustrates this truth well.

He tells us of a shepherd who, realizing one sheep was lost, was willing to leave ninety-nine to seek it. No creature strays more easily than a sheep. Yet the shepherd valued the sheep.

The sheep was a priority to the shepherd, and it caused him to leave the flock. Likewise, if lost souls are a priority to us, we will leave our comfort. No one ever rescued a sheep from his living room, and no one ever rescued a soul without inconveniencing himself.

Several years ago, *TIME* magazine carried a story about former president George H. Bush returning to the South Pacific Island of Chichi-jima, where two of his crewmen were killed in the crash of his Avenger torpedo bomber. From a low-flying helicopter, he dropped wreaths over the approximate spot of their ocean graves and then went on shore. *TIME* reports:

> On Chichi-jima Bush met a former Japanese soldier who claimed he actually saw the rescue of Bush when the submarine Finback surfaced and plucked him off his tiny dinghy. The old man related that one of his friends had remarked as they watched the swift rescue, "Surely America will win the war if they care so much for the life of one pilot."[2]

As we schedule our priorities, may we never forget the value of one soul.

WHEN IT'S INCONVENIENT

It's not always easy to go soulwinning, and it's definitely not always comfortable. Evangelist John R. Rice observed, "The best soulwinners are those who go when it is convenient and then go when it is not convenient."[3]

For many Christians, it's not that they wouldn't be willing to witness for Christ. It's just that they have other goals. And taking time to share the gospel does not advance those goals. Basically, it's inconvenient.

Having the ability to help yet withholding help is the most inhumane thing in the world to do. Imagine Jonas Salk withholding the polio vaccination. Or imagine seeing a drowning man and neglecting to rescue him.

This is exactly what Missionary Hudson Taylor saw. His son and daughter-in-law related the story:

…he was travelling by native junk from Shanghai to Ningpo. Among his fellow-passengers, one Chinese, who had spent some years in England and went by the name of Peter, was much upon his heart, for, though not unacquainted with the Gospel, he knew nothing of its saving power. Simply he told the story of this man's friendliness and of his own efforts to win him to Christ. Nearing the city of Sung-kiang, they were preparing to go ashore together to preach and distribute tracts, when Mr. Taylor in his cabin was startled by a sudden splash and cry that told of a man overboard. Springing at once on deck he looked round and missed Peter.

"Yes," exclaimed the boatmen unconcernedly, "it was over there he went down!"

To drop the sail and jump into the water was the work of a moment; but the tide was running out, and the low, shrubless shore afforded little landmark. Searching everywhere in an agony of suspense, Mr. Taylor caught sight of some fishermen with a drag-net—just the thing needed.

"Come," he cried as hope revived, "come and drag over this spot. A man is drowning!"

"Veh bin," was the amazing reply: "It is not convenient."

"Don't talk of convenience! Quickly come, or it will be too late."

"We are busy fishing."

"Never mind your fishing! Come—only come at once! I will pay you well."

"How much will you give us?"

"Five dollars! Only don't stand talking. Save life without delay!"

"Too little!" they shouted across the water. "We will not come for less than thirty dollars."

"But I have not so much with me. I will give you all I've got."

"And how much may that be?"

"Oh, I don't know. About fourteen dollars."

Upon this they came, and the first time they passed the net through the water brought up the missing man. But all Mr. Taylor's efforts to restore respiration were in vain. It was only too plain that life had fled, sacrificed to the callous indifference of those who might easily have saved it.

A burning sense of indignation swept over the great audience. Could it be that anywhere on earth people were to be found so utterly callous and selfish! But as the earnest voice went on, conviction struck home all the more deeply that it was unexpected.

"Is the body, then, of so much more value than the soul? We condemn those heathen fishermen. We say they were guilty of the man's death—because they could easily have saved him, and did not do it. But what of the millions whom we leave to perish, and that eternally? What of the plain command, 'Go ye into all the world and preach the gospel to every creature,' and the searching question inspired by God Himself: 'If thou forbear to deliver them that are drawn unto death, and those that are ready to be slain; if thou sayest, Behold, we knew it not; doth not He that pondereth the heart consider it? and He that keepeth thy soul doth not He know it? And shall He not render to every man according to his works?'"[4]

This story makes *convenience* a word to shudder at. "We're busy" either means "We don't see the need" or "We don't care about the need." I'm afraid that too often it means both.

Do we believe that the greatest need in the world is salvation? Do we believe Christ cares about the people around us—our neighbors, for instance? Then what have we done to share the gospel with them? I worry about a people who will not be inconvenienced for the gospel. Perhaps we have forgotten what is truly important.

SPIRITUAL INTERVENTION

Crops go through three stages: green, ripe, and rotten. Harvest is only effective during the ripe stage. In soulwinning, we never know when someone is at that stage. Often, we think he is not ready yet or wouldn't be interested in the gospel. But it very well may be that God has already been preparing his heart to respond to the gospel. The spiritual intervention of our witnessing to a lost soul at just the right time can produce a rich spiritual harvest.

John Downey was such a man. I remember the day I met him as I shook his hand after a Sunday morning church service. At the exact moment I asked him if I could come by to see him that week, he was asking me if I would come by to talk.

John had quite a backstory. He was raised Catholic, but seeing the deadness of empty religion turned him away. As soon as he was eighteen, he was done with church.

And yet, God wasn't done with John. Over the following years, God continued bringing people into his life to sow the seed of God's Word, and He brought trials into his life to open his heart to that seed.

When John's twenty-six-year-old wife was killed in a car accident, John became angry and bitter. Left with two young daughters and deeply missing his wife, John was sure God was out to get him. His mother-in-law, however, wasn't so sure. She sent John a Bible and told him that God's promises would help him to get through those dark days. She also told him that his wife had trusted Christ as her Saviour as a fourteen-year-old girl. Although John appreciated the gesture of kindness, he didn't budge. He didn't want to give up his anger toward God.

In time, John met Laura, a young, single mom with a daughter of her own. John and Laura easily fell in love. As they discussed marriage and blending their families, John blurted out, "I'll tell you one thing, we're not going to the Catholic church." That wasn't a problem to Laura as she had not been raised Catholic. In fact, she told him then that she had trusted Christ as her personal Saviour when she was a child. John didn't say much, but he remembered what his mother-in-law had told him, and he filed the information away in his mind. John and Laura married, and their lives moved forward.

Around this same time, our church began our first bus route, picking up children whose parents would allow them to come but who didn't come themselves. As God would orchestrate it, two bus workers knocked on the Downeys' door and talked to John and Laura's three girls. They must have been pretty convincing in their invitation because when John came home from work that evening, the girls begged him to let them ride the bus to the Baptist church.

Something clicked in John's heart when his girls asked him to let them go to church—and that something was a work of God. Suddenly, he realized his spiritual responsibility toward his daughters. "Actually," he told them, "I think God's telling *me* to take you to church." The girls were surprised but excited.

They didn't go the next day, however, or the next Sunday… or the week after. In fact, several weeks passed. Then one Sunday morning, John woke up with a definite conviction on his heart that he needed to bring his family to church. He told Laura, who was surprised but thankful. Together they got the girls ready.

There was no doubt in John's mind where they would be going to church. He had already established that it would not be the Catholic church, and he still had the invitation the bus workers had brought to the house. Less than three hours after John woke up that morning, the Downey family was seated on the second row of Lancaster Baptist Church. He listened intently to the preaching, but he did not respond to the invitation at the end of the message to trust Christ. He still had too much to sort through in his mind.

That Tuesday evening, soulwinners from our church stopped by the Downey home, but the timing wasn't right to ask John about his salvation. Their visit, however, did encourage the Downeys to return the following Sunday. It was after the service that Sunday that John and I set an appointment for the following Tuesday evening.

There in the Downeys' living room, as I opened my Bible and shared the gospel, John trusted Christ as his Saviour. The seeds that had been planted in his heart by his mother-in-law, Laura's testimony, and the messages in church finally took root.

And have those seeds ever produced a rich harvest! John was saved in November of 1987, and within weeks of his salvation he began sharing the gospel with others. Six months later, he was introduced to the bus ministry where he has served now for over twenty-five years. It's not uncommon today for me to ask a newcomer to Lancaster Baptist how they came to the church and for them to answer, "I was saved as a child when I rode Brother Downey's bus…."

Through the bus ministry, door-to-door soulwinning, and talking to friends, neighbors, and acquaintances, John is still soulwinning consistently and leading others to Christ regularly. All of this is due to seeds of the gospel planted and watered by faithful soulwinners and germinated by the Holy Spirit. To this day, those seeds continue to multiply into an abundant spiritual harvest—a testimony to what can happen when we will make Christ's command our priority.

HIS LAST COMMAND

I don't know who said it first, but I love the quote, "His last command must be our first priority." The men and women who have been greatly used of God have been people who have made Christ's command their first priority. The "great Christians" of the past who we remember today were diligent personal soulwinners. They were men and women who so grasped the priorities of Christ that those priorities gripped them.

We saw a moment ago that Hudson Taylor was such a man. But Taylor didn't magically become a soulwinner by going to the mission field. Read his autobiography, *A Ribbon of Blue*, and you'll see that he was a soulwinner years before he went to China. He was a soulwinner as a pharmacist, as a medical student—in every occupation he found himself and in every place he went.

It was Taylor who so pointedly stated, "The great commission is not an option to be considered; it is a command to be obeyed."

Yes, the command of Christ is a *Great* Commission. Actually, it is the great*est* commission. It is the opportunity to be engaged in the incredible redemption plan of God.

And it's not an option. It's a command.

I don't merely believe in the concept of soulwinning; I believe it is the heart of Jesus for the local church. Looking at the vast majority of Christian activity today, however, I'd say we treat the Great Commission more like an option.

We have lots of programs, resources, and opportunities available in the local church. But how often are we actively sharing the gospel with the lost?

This *is* our commission. It is not our option—it is our command.

And it must be our priority.

A CHURCH-WIDE PRIORITY

Across America, there are fewer and fewer soulwinning churches. And it's not because the few who evangelize are doing such a good job that there's no need for more. On the contrary, it's because we've gotten comfortable in our priorities and ignored Christ's command.

The average church today is like a social club, not an organized body of believers intent on obeying Christ's command. Too many Christians are content to treat evangelism like a football game—in which they are the spectators.

My friend, we *must* change our priorities. Jesus came to seek and to save the lost, and when He left, He commissioned us to continue.

We need to seriously face the rebuke of Proverbs 10:5: "He that sleepeth in harvest is a son that causeth shame."

On the other hand, we can seriously claim God's promise to bless our labors when we are faithful in our priorities. First Corinthians 3:6 tells us that when we plant the seed of the gospel, and water that seed, God will give the increase: "I have planted, Apollos watered; but God gave the increase."

Too often, the average churchgoer finds himself a *loiterer,* rather than a *laborer.* He just sort of hangs around, watching. But God has called us to a mission. As long as there is a ready harvest around us, that harvest is our priority.

FIRST THINGS SECOND?

Perhaps in your heart of hearts, you believe the Great Commission is your priority. But if you want to know what in actuality is your priority, there are two easy places to look: your to-do list and your schedule.

I think an honest look at the schedules of most Christians today contrasted with the urgency of the Great Commission would reveal an uncomfortable diagnosis: we've made Christ's priorities our options.

Jesus said, "Seek ye *first* the kingdom of God..." (Matthew 6:33). We're happy to seek the advancement of His kingdom...if we have time. More often than not, however, we only seem to have time to seek it second or third...or not at all.

Our schedules are always full. There are always important responsibilities and opportunities clamoring for our attention. But at some point, we have to step back and say, "I must work the works of him that sent me, while it is day: the night cometh, when no man can work" (John 9:4). At some point, we have to say, "Evangelism is my priority, and I'm going to make it happen."

Like you, I have a full to do list. (I even have a "someday/maybe list" for the projects that I know won't make it on my to do list.) And like you, not everything on my list gets done. Sometimes I never move past the first few items.

This is why evangelism must be our first item. I urge you, don't say, "I'll get around to it." Decide that you will do it.

There are some things that we make time for. And I believe the Great Commission of Christ should be at the top of that list.

The mandate of Christ is an active mandate. He simply said, "Go."

Do you want to go? Make time for it. Schedule it.

Living by priorities means that we have to let some things go. But it means we make those as purposeful decisions, not as regretful happenchance. It means we decide what we are going to let go and that this letting-go list does not include Christ's last command to the local church.

From the very beginning of Christ's ministry, He called men to turn from their pursuits and follow Him: "Now as he walked by the sea of Galilee, he saw Simon and Andrew his brother casting a net into the sea: for they were fishers. And Jesus said unto them, Come ye after me, and I will make you to become fishers of men" (Mark 1:16–17).

What do you need to turn from—or at least bump down on your priority list—to follow Christ in reaching the souls of men?

OBEDIENT HUSTLE

I know that soulwinning is not our only priority. Indeed, God has given me a family to love and provide for and a church family to lead and disciple. All of us live in a constant balancing act of managing our God-given responsibilities. So please understand, I'm not suggesting you put this book down immediately and begin knocking on doors in your town like a wild man. But how *do* we balance the weight of the need with our many responsibilities?

One word: obedience. We simply obey what Christ has commanded us to do. We put it on top of our schedule.

And we hustle. Not panic, hustle.

We hustle in the same way I wanted my future sons-in-law to prepare for marriage. I didn't want them wildly trying to earn money to support my daughters, but I did want them to get busy. I didn't want them to let grass grow under their feet.

This was the response of Jesus toward the Father's business: "And he said unto them, How is it that ye sought me? wist ye not that I must be about my Father's business?" (Luke 2:49).

Must.

Hustle.

So how do you do it? I can't end a chapter like this—a chapter on action—without giving you some practical to dos. We already established that soulwinning is our highest priority, so these to dos should be high on your list.

What can you do to make soulwinning a priority?

1. Seek the fullness of the Holy Spirit. There is no strategy, method, or action plan that can make up for a lack of the Holy Spirit's power. Before we even begin to think of programs or ideas to reach people with the gospel, we must follow the most basic instruction to fully yield ourselves to the Holy Spirit. (We'll look at this more fully in Chapter 8.)

2. Become soul-conscious. Scheduling a weekly time to go witnessing is the easy part. Developing a consciousness of eternity and the souls around us takes effort. (Invariably, however, "going soulwinning" heightens my sensitivity to the spiritual needs around me.)

3. Purposefully develop relationships. Sometimes in our zeal to get gospel presentations out, we neglect to nurture relationships with our neighbors, coworkers, teachers, barbers/ hair stylists, or extended family members. Presenting the gospel at someone's doorstep is biblical, and I've seen many people respond to Christ at the door. But sharing Christ's offer of salvation with someone with whom you already have a relationship is also biblical. Nurture the relationships you have, and look for opportunities to share Christ. (For an idea on a church-wide effort to develop soulwinning-focused relationships, see Chapter 15.)

4. Pursue soulwinning as a discipline. I realize that our soulwinning efforts should not be restricted to a brief weekly time or a public setting. We should be soulwinners twenty-four hours a day, seven days a week—always ready to give an answer for the hope that is within us. But I also believe that if we are to make personal soulwinning a priority in our lives, we must be disciplined and predetermined. We must put a plan into place for how and when we will obey this command of Christ. Schedule specific soulwinning times, systematically work through a map of your community, and keep an active prospect list for follow up. (For detailed instructions on a plan that has worked well for our church over the years, see Chapter 12.)

5. Write your action plan. This step should be the outflow of the steps above. Similar to wisely crafted New Year's goals, this plan is your statement of intent for a particular season of ministry (perhaps the fall or an entire year), and it will be the basis for your time management. It should include your priorities and regular commitments as well as your personal goals for outreach.

I tend to do this exercise in the fall because this is the strongest season of our church outreach. Each fall, I set goals for soulwinning outreach, and I ask the Holy Spirit to allow me to see a number of families saved, baptized, and enrolled in our church's formal discipleship program. As a pastor, I also have goals for our church of involving more members in soulwinning and helping each member of our church family to grow in personal fruitfulness.

Without an action plan, you become a prisoner of events. But with an action plan, your events have purpose.

ETERNAL PRIORITIES, ETERNAL REWARDS

When we make Christ's command our priority, when we structure our lives around the priorities of eternity, we receive an incredible bonus—eternal rewards.

At the end of life, our greatest joy will be the rewards of our eternal investments of time. Paul often expressed that those he had led to Christ and spiritually nurtured in discipleship were his "joy and crown"—his trophy.

> *For what is our hope, or joy, or crown of rejoicing? Are not even ye in the presence of our Lord Jesus Christ at his coming?*—1 THESSALONIANS 2:19

> *Therefore, my brethren dearly beloved and longed for, my joy and crown, so stand fast in the Lord, my dearly beloved.*—PHILIPPIANS 4:1

Eternal priorities bring eternal rewards. What a joy it will be to stand before Christ with the fruit of souls! It will only happen, however, if we insist on placing in our lives the priorities of Christ—as we make His last command our first priority, His great commission our greatest mission.

---

1   John W. Stott, "*The Great Commission*," in *One Race, One Gospel, One Task*, ed. Carl F. Henry and W. Stanley Mooneyham (World Wide Publications, 1967), 1:46.

2   Hugh Sidey, "One Bush's War and Remembrance" (TIME Magazine, September 15, 2002), http://content.time.com/time/magazine/article/0,9171,351225,00.html.

3   John R. Rice, *Soul Winning* (Sword of the Lord Publishers, 1944), 20.

4   Dr. and Mrs. Howard Taylor, *Hudson Taylor and the China Inland Mission: The Growth of a Work of God* (OMF International, formerly China Inland Mission, first printing 1918, this printing 2000), 4–6.

SEVEN

THE FILLING
OF A SOULWINNER

Have you ever considered the impossibility of leading a single soul to Christ? I have—every time I attempt to do it.

As much as I believe in soulwinning, and as obvious as is Christ's command for us to do it, there is something we must understand about it—we *can't* do it.

I can't convict a person of sin.

I can't change a heart.

I can't convince a person to place his faith in Christ.

Thankfully, I don't have to. And neither do you.

SPIRITUAL FRUIT AND THE REAL SOULWINNER

On Christ's last evening with His disciples, He told them, "Ye have not chosen me, but I have chosen you, and ordained you, that ye should go and bring forth fruit, and that your fruit should remain: that whatsoever ye shall ask of the Father in my name, he may give it you" (John 15:16).

Ordained simply speaks of being set apart for a purpose. I remember when I was ordained into the gospel ministry in 1983. Pastors and deacons laid hands on me and prayed for me, and I was set apart for the purpose of preaching the gospel. But Christ tells us that He has chosen and ordained each of us—every Christian—to bear fruit for Him.

But we must understand: we *cannot* bear lasting spiritual fruit on our own. Jesus told His disciples, "I am the vine, ye are the branches: He that abideth in me, and I in him, the same bringeth forth much fruit: for without me ye can do nothing" (John 15:5).

Without Him, we can do nothing.

Zilch.

Nada.

Without the filling of the Holy Spirit, we'll make up our own programs and fabricate our own "fruit." We'll gain followers, but they will be our disciples, not His. And our fruit won't possibly remain.

NEVER ALONE

As Christ commissioned His disciples to take the gospel into all the world, He assured them, "…lo, I am with you alway, even unto the end of the world. Amen" (Matthew 28:20).

We do not face the task of reaching the world alone—Christ's power is available to us. And it is the Holy Spirit who imparts that power to us.

In the same conversation that Christ told His disciples they could do nothing without Him and that He had called them to bear fruit for Him, He promised them help: "Nevertheless I tell you the truth; It is expedient for you that I go away: for if I go not away, the Comforter will not come unto you; but if I depart, I will send him unto you. And when he is come, he will reprove the world of sin, and of righteousness, and of judgment: Of sin, because they believe not on me" (John 16:7–9). Only the Holy Spirit can convict people of their need for Christ and convince them to place their faith in Him. If we are to obey Christ's commission to preach the gospel, we need the Holy Spirit's power.

In Acts 1:8, Christ promised His disciples that the Holy Spirit would enable them to witness for Him: "But ye shall receive power, after that the Holy Ghost is come upon you: and ye shall be witnesses unto me...."

The task before us—to evangelize the world—is great. But the power within us—the Holy Spirit of God—is greater!

DANGEROUS SUBSTITUTES

With the power of the Holy Spirit within, why is our task not completed?

There are many answers to this question, and they all relate to either neglecting our task entirely or substituting our power for the Holy Spirit's power. Sometimes we do this even as we proactively engage in soulwinning.

I believe it is vital that we schedule time to go soulwinning, and I believe in having a systematic plan in place to reach our communities with the gospel. But in all of our planning and scheduling, there is a danger—that we would forget our programs are not a substitute for the Holy Spirit. Sometimes we create systems, means, methods, plans, and strategies that could require little of the power of God. We must rely on His power, not our methods.

Charles Spurgeon said it eloquently: "Without the Spirit of God we can do nothing; we are as ships without wind, or chariots without steeds; like branches without sap, we are withered; like coals without fire, we are useless; as an offering without the sacrificial flame, we are unaccepted."[1]

In the coming chapters, we'll look at systems, programs, and charts to help with evangelism. I believe all of these are beneficial tools. But remember, none of these can substitute for the power of God in our lives. None of these can substitute for a pure life in which the Holy Spirit is free to work, a surrendered heart to which the Holy Spirit speaks, or a responsive will through which the Holy Spirit acts.

Simply put, not only do we need the Holy Spirit as the "Real Soulwinner," but we need to be yielded to Him.

EMPTY TO BE FULL

Scripture teaches us that the Holy Spirit indwells all believers at the moment of salvation. Ephesians 1:13 tells us that we are "sealed with that holy Spirit of promise," and 1 Corinthians 6:19 explains, "your body is the temple of the Holy Ghost which is in you." What a gift—the very presence of God within!

It is important to understand, however, that there is a difference between *having* the Holy Spirit and being *filled* with the Holy Spirit. Ephesians 5:18 instructs, "And be not drunk with wine, wherein is excess; but be filled with the Spirit." When we are saved, the Holy Spirit gives Himself to us, but it is then our choice to give ourselves to Him in willing surrender.

To "be filled with" means "to be controlled by." Just as a drunken person is controlled by alcohol, so a spiritual Christian is controlled by the Holy Spirit.

What does this look like in everyday living?

Three words describe it best: transparency, surrender, and responsiveness.

Transparency means my heart is open to the Holy Spirit's conviction in my life—that there is an authenticity in my relationship with Him. It means I ask Him to search my heart and life for anything—attitudes, words, actions, activities—that is displeasing to Him. David prayed, "Search me, O God, and know my heart: try me, and know my thoughts: And see if there be any wicked way in me, and lead me in the way everlasting" (Psalm 139:23–24).

Surrender means my heart is yielded to the Holy Spirit's commands—that I'm unwilling to quench His working in my life by stubbornness. It means that in my heart I've already determined that any command or principle I see in God's Word relative to any part of my life, I'm going to obey. First Thessalonians 5:19 commands us, "Quench not the Spirit."

We can't live on our own terms, ignoring God's commands for our lives, and then quickly ask God for His Spirit's power before we make door-to-door soulwinning visits. Being filled with the Spirit only happens as we are surrendered to Him in all areas of our lives.

Responsiveness means my heart is sensitive to and ready to answer the Holy Spirit's promptings—that whenever and wherever I am I will respond to His inner prompting to witness for Him. Beyond being yielded to the Holy Spirit in each area of life, I must be obedient to His promptings to witness. Some Christians treat soulwinning as if it were only a scheduled activity. I am all for scheduling soulwinning, but I don't *only* believe in soulwinning on schedule. I believe we should make time for (i.e. schedule) the greatest work in the entire world, but I also believe we must be responsive to the Holy Spirit when He brings souls to us!

We see both patterns throughout the New Testament. Paul systematically taught "publickly, and from house to house" (Acts 20:20), but he also responsively "disputed…in the synagogue with the Jews, and with the devout persons, and in the market daily" as well as taking the opportunity to preach on Mars' hill while he was waiting in Athens during a non-scheduled time (Acts 17:16–19).

Simply put, being "filled with" the Holy Spirit is not something we turn on and off. It's a full-time transparent surrender and responsiveness to the Holy Spirit of God. When we thus yield to Him, He works in and through us in ways that are beyond our power to conceive.

One of my favorite testimonies of that is of Stephen Grellet—an American businessman in the nineteenth century who knew what it was to obey the prompting of the Holy Spirit to witness. The story is told of how he once sensed the Lord directing him to preach the gospel in a certain lumber camp in the backwoods of Canada. With nothing but an unmistakable conviction that God told him to go, he made the journey northward to the camp.

Arriving at the camp, Grellet discovered that it had been deserted. Sure, however, that the Holy Spirit had directed him there to preach, he preached the gospel to the tree stumps. With nothing left to do, he made his return trip home.

Many years later, a stranger approached Grellet and asked him if he were indeed Stephen Grellet. The stranger then explained that years ago, he had been part of a lumber crew in Canada. After one of the moves the crew had made from one camp to the next, the foreman of the crew had sent this worker back to camp to retrieve an article that had been left behind. As the worker approached the camp, he heard as it were a voice from Heaven. Shocked and frightened, because he knew the camp was empty, he hid and listened. In those moments, he heard Stephen Grellet preach the gospel of Christ, and as he meditated on the Scriptures in the days following, he trusted Christ as his personal Saviour.[2]

I've never preached to an empty lumber camp or had quite so dramatic a salvation testimony shared with me, but I have seen time and again the Lord bless my obedience when I am right with Him and obedient to His prompting to witness for Him.

FILLED EQUALS FRUITFUL

When it comes to being filled with the Holy Spirit, Scripture presents a simple equation:

Christian - self + filled with the Spirit = fruitful witness

Being filled with the Holy Spirit *will* result in fruitfulness in our witness. We may not see the fruit immediately (such as in Stephen Grellet's case); we may not even see all of it until eternity. But if we are yielded to the Holy Spirit, we *will* witness of Christ, and we *will* have fruit that remains for Christ.

It's a win-win proposition. We surrender self to enjoy His presence and power, and we get to bear the fruit that we were created to bear for Him.

How we bear that fruit is the subject of our next chapter.

----

1   Charles Spurgeon, quoted by Warren Wiersbe in *Classic Sermons on Revival and Spiritual Renewal* (Kregel Publications, 1995), 46.

2   Lee Roberson, *The Gold Mine* (Sword of the Lord Publishers, 1996), 75.

EIGHT

THE MESSAGE
OF A SOULWINNER

Throughout the pages of Scripture, the Holy Spirit gives many analogies for the work of a soulwinner. It is likened to a shepherd seeking a lost sheep (Luke 15:4–7), a farmer harvesting his crops (John 4:35–36), and a fisherman bringing in the fish (Luke 5:10). Another analogy is that of an ambassador who is sent with a message:

> *And all things are of God, who hath reconciled us to himself by Jesus Christ, and hath given to us the ministry of reconciliation; To wit, that God was in Christ, reconciling the world unto himself, not imputing their trespasses unto them; and hath committed unto us the word of reconciliation. Now then we are ambassadors for Christ, as though God did beseech you by us: we pray you in Christ's stead, be ye reconciled to God.*
> —2 CORINTHIANS 5:18–20

This message with which we—God's ambassadors—have been entrusted is vital. It is the message of reconciliation to God. It is a matter of eternal life or eternal death. It is a message which we must deliver, and it is a message which we must deliver with clarity.

THE GOSPEL, PURE AND SIMPLE

What exactly is this message we bring? Paul wrote to the church in Corinth, "Moreover, brethren, I declare unto you the gospel which I preached unto you, which also ye have received, and wherein ye stand" (1 Corinthians 15:1). A few verses later, Paul spelled out the gospel in a nutshell:

> *For I delivered unto you first of all that which I also received, how that Christ died for our sins according to the scriptures; And that he was buried, and that he rose again the third day according to the scriptures:*
> —1 CORINTHIANS 15:3–4

That is the gospel—the death, burial, and resurrection of Christ for our sins.

The word *gospel* literally means "good news." Indeed, Christ's death in our stead, His burial, and His triumphant victory over the grave *is* good news! By placing our trust in Him and in the payment He already paid for our sins, we are reconciled to God and given a home in Heaven. This is the message of the soulwinner.

Some people complicate this message. They so front-load it with elaborate terminology and extra-biblical requirements that it becomes more of a discussion point among mature Christians than a gospel invitation to the lost. In truth, volumes could be written on the doctrines of salvation. However, those of us who have shared the gospel with lost people and have seen many come to Christ know that no one understands all the theology behind salvation the day they are saved. Nor do they need to. They simply need to understand the gospel itself—and turn in faith to Christ.

While some complicate the message, others make it shallow. They are repetitive and trite in their presentation, making it more of a sales pitch to "pray a prayer" than a call to turn in repentance and believe solely in Christ for salvation. Shallow presentations of the gospel tend to yield professions of salvation with no fruit of changed lives.

Both extremes—the complicated, front-loaded requirements and the shallow, trite presentations—garble the message with which we have been entrusted. We must learn to share the gospel in its pure simplicity while relying on the Holy Spirit to convict hearts and to be the true Soulwinner.

A MESSAGE, NOT A SCRIPT

Let's say you really were sworn into office as an ambassador of the United States of America. Let's say you were commissioned to go to a country whose intents could be hostile, but you are sent with a peace offer that is generous and gracious. And let's say you go as a solo ambassador.

I'm guessing that before you go, you'll study—inside and out, backwards and forwards—the message you carry. You'll probably go to the meetings with a prewritten speech—or at least an outline. But behind that speech, you'll know the message you seek to convey.

Let's imagine that as you delve into your speech, you notice your listeners aren't responding. They've tuned you out, or they've misunderstood what you've said. What will you do now? You'll lay the speech aside and with the message that is burning in your heart try to think of every possible way to lodge your message in their hearts and persuade them to agree with you. You know the stakes are high, and you care more about the message than you do following a predetermined presentation.

You and I *are* ambassadors—for Christ. We've been entrusted with the most important message in the world, and we are to deliver it in a way so as to connect it with hearts. Second Corinthians 5:20 goes so far as to say, "we are ambassadors for Christ, *as though God did beseech you by us:* we pray you in Christ's stead, be ye reconciled to God."

How do we handle such a vital message? First, we begin with an "outline"—some kind of plan in how we will present the message. We don't take a message carrying the importance of the gospel and simply "wing it" each time we have the opportunity to witness for Christ. What I am going to give you in this chapter is something like an outline. It is a basic structure including key Scripture verses that you can use to share the gospel with another person.

But even as you learn this outline, remember to let your heart and mind be saturated, not so much with the order of the outline, but with the gospel itself (the death, burial, and resurrection of Christ for our sins) and the importance of communicating that message to your listener.

You and I have an advantage in delivering our message that no political ambassador sent on behalf of another can claim. We have the Originator of the message—the Holy Spirit—indwelling us. And we have His promise to guide and direct us. John 16:13 says, "Howbeit when he, the Spirit of truth, is come, he will guide you into all truth: for he shall not speak of himself; but whatsoever he shall hear, that shall he speak: and he will shew you things to come." Although this verse tells us the Holy Spirit will direct us *personally* to the truths we need from God's Word, it is also a promise that He will direct us as we seek to point *others* to Christ.

As you share the gospel message with others, remember to let the Holy Spirit lead you. Remember, He is the real soulwinner. You and I are simply message-bearers. He is the one who convicts people of sin and points them to Christ. We are the ones who have the privilege of sharing the Scriptures that He uses.

BASIC GOSPEL SCRIPTURES

Acts 8 records the story of Philip leading a man we often refer to as "the Ethiopian eunuch" to Christ. It's a fascinating account of a Spirit-filled soulwinner responding to the questions of a Spirit-prepared listener.

> *And the angel of the Lord spake unto Philip, saying, Arise, and go toward the south unto the way that goeth*

down from Jerusalem unto Gaza, which is desert. And he arose and went: and, behold, a man of Ethiopia, an eunuch of great authority under Candace queen of the Ethiopians, who had the charge of all her treasure, and had come to Jerusalem for to worship, Was returning, and sitting in his chariot read Esaias the prophet. Then the Spirit said unto Philip, Go near, and join thyself to this chariot. And Philip ran thither to him, and heard him read the prophet Esaias, and said, Understandest thou what thou readest? And he said, How can I, except some man should guide me? And he desired Philip that he would come up and sit with him. The place of the scripture which he read was this, He was led as a sheep to the slaughter; and like a lamb dumb before his shearer, so opened he not his mouth: In his humiliation his judgment was taken away: and who shall declare his generation? for his life is taken from the earth. And the eunuch answered Philip, and said, I pray thee, of whom speaketh the prophet this? of himself, or of some other man? Then Philip opened his mouth, and began at the same scripture, and preached unto him Jesus. And as they went on their way, they came unto a certain water: and the eunuch said, See, here is water; what doth hinder me to be baptized? And Philip said, If thou believest with all thine heart, thou mayest. And he answered and said, I believe that Jesus Christ is the Son of God.—ACTS 8:26–37

I love this passage because it demonstrates that the Holy Spirit prepares the hearts of those whom we would consider unlikely to respond to the gospel, and He uses His Word to work in hearts.

Prior to this desert soulwinning experience, Philip had been preaching the gospel in Samaria. I would imagine that Philip preached there from a different Scripture passage than the passage he used with the Ethiopian. And yet, Philip, who thoroughly understood the gospel in its glorious simplicity was able to "at the same scripture" where the Ethiopian was reading "preach unto him Jesus."

This is why we must understand the message we share and be sensitive to the promptings of the Holy Spirit. If we reduce the gospel message to a predetermined set of verses and explanations, we miss opportunities to follow the leadership of the Holy Spirit and speak directly to the issues where He is already working in a lost person's heart.

That said, there *are* a core set of verses, often called "the Romans Road" (because they are from the book of Romans), that clearly give the main truths of the gospel—that we are sinners condemned by God, that Christ died for our sins, and that He offers us the gift of salvation.

My advice to new soulwinners is to learn and memorize these verses and to be prepared to share them with a lost person in any setting—out doorknocking, with a friend over a cup of coffee, etc. You may even want to mark the verses in your New Testament so they are easy for you to find as you witness.

My advice to all soulwinners, however, is to let the Holy Spirit lead you in which Scriptures to use as you share the gospel. While having a starting place is important and the Romans Road is a clear way to share the gospel, realize that the Holy Spirit will lead you to use other Scriptures. Listen to the person with whom you are speaking, and as you grow as a Christian, you should also be growing as a soulwinner in your ability to use other passages of Scripture as needed in your soulwinning. As we saw in Philip's presentation of the gospel to the Ethiopian, the message of the gospel is all throughout Scripture. It is not limited only to a handful of verses in the book of Romans!

But, for a basic framework, the four main truths and the verses below provide a good start for sharing the gospel with someone who is lost. I will often ask the person a question to open dialog. Depending on the context of the situation, I may ask, "Has anyone shown you from the Bible how you can know without a doubt you are on your way to Heaven?" or "If you were to die today, do you know if you would go to Heaven or Hell or do you know?" If they are not sure, I ask if they will allow me a few moments to share what the Bible says. These are the basic truths I share from Scripture:

REALIZE YOUR CONDITION

As it is written, There is none righteous, no, not one: —Romans 3:10

For all have sinned, and come short of the glory of God;—Romans 3:23

All of us have a sin nature, and all of us sin by choice. Sin is any act contrary to God's laws and commandments, and our sin separates us from God.

(If the person with whom I'm speaking has a religious background and is familiar with the basic story of Adam and Eve, I will also point them to Romans 5:12: "Wherefore, as by one man sin entered into the world, and death by sin; and so death passed upon all men, for that all have sinned.")

NOTICE GOD'S PRICE FOR SIN

For the wages of sin is death; but the gift of God is eternal life through Jesus Christ our Lord.—ROMANS 6:23

A wage is what you earn by what you do. For instance, a man earns a paycheck for the work he has done. Even so, we have earned eternal death in Hell for the sins we have committed.

REALIZE THAT CHRIST DIED FOR YOU

But God commendeth [showed] his love toward us, in that, while we were yet sinners, Christ died for us.
—ROMANS 5:8

We deserve eternal death for our sin, but Jesus paid our payment when He died for us. Although we were lost and separated from God, He loved us. Because He is love, He sent His own Son—Jesus Christ—to die on the cross for our sin. After His death, He rose from the dead three days later.

John 3:16 explains, "For God so loved the world, that he gave his only begotten Son, that whosoever believeth in him should not perish, but have everlasting life."

Through His death and resurrection, Jesus became the payment for our sin. Now we do not have to pay for our sin ourselves. By His grace, salvation is provided.

As Romans 6:23 tells us, Christ now offers us the gift of eternal life: "…the gift of God is eternal life through Jesus Christ our Lord." This is a gift Christ paid for when He died for our sins.

CONFESS YOUR FAITH IN CHRIST

To have a relationship with God and an eternal home in Heaven, we must stop trusting ourselves, our works, or our religion and place our full trust in the Lord Jesus Christ alone for forgiveness of our sin and for eternal life.

> *That if thou shalt confess with thy mouth the Lord Jesus, and shalt believe in thine heart that God hath raised him from the dead, thou shalt be saved. For with the heart man believeth unto righteousness; and with the mouth confession is made unto salvation. For the scripture saith, Whosoever believeth on him shall not be ashamed.*—ROMANS 10:9–11

To "be saved" speaks of being saved from the penalty of our sins—eternal separation from God in Hell. Although we are sinners separated from God, Jesus Christ—the perfect, sinless, Son of God—provided the way of salvation.

God Himself promises that if you realize your sinful condition and will confess Christ as your Saviour, trusting the payment He made for your sin and turning to Him alone to be your Saviour, He will save you.

> *For whosoever shall call upon the name of the Lord shall be saved.*—ROMANS 10:13

(At this point, I am very sensitive to how the person is responding. If he has been attentive and it seems the Holy Spirit is working conviction in his heart, I'll continue our conversation by inviting him to call on the Lord Jesus by faith for salvation.

But if he's distracted and only giving cursory mental assent to these truths, I'll likely pull back and give the Holy Spirit time to work in his heart. I'll still try to keep in contact with him, and I'll look for another opportunity to witness to him. If I continue, I'll likely ask a few summary questions, something like the following.)

- Do you believe that you are a sinner, separated from God, and without the ability to save yourself?
- Do you believe that Jesus, God's Son, shed His blood to pay for your sin?
- Would there be anything that would keep you from turning to and trusting in Jesus Christ as your Saviour today?

As we saw a moment ago, God promises, "That if thou shalt confess with thy mouth the Lord Jesus, and shalt believe in thine heart that God hath raised him from the dead, thou shalt be saved. For with the heart man believeth unto righteousness; and with the mouth confession is made unto salvation. For whosoever shall call upon the name of the Lord shall be saved" (Romans 10:9–10, 13).

Even as you "confess with your mouth" that you are putting your trust in Christ, it is important that you also "believe in your heart." It is the faith of your heart that saves you.

(At this point, I ask, "Would you like to turn to Christ in faith and call on the Lord for salvation now?" If they reply with a "yes," I typically review the gospel presentation in the form of a prayer. I remind them that they are talking to God in prayer, and they should confess to Him their sin and ask Him, as the

Son of God, to cleanse them from sin and be their Saviour. I invite them then to pray for salvation.)

ADDITIONAL THOUGHTS ON PRESENTING THE GOSPEL

The verses and brief explanations above are a very basic outline for sharing the gospel. But I'd like to admonish you again that as you grow as a Christian and as a soulwinner, be flexible in your presentation if someone is not understanding the gospel or if they have a question or if the Holy Spirit directs you to share another passage of Scripture.

After having shared the gospel, some soulwinners will ask a person to repeat a prayer after them. I have done this on a few occasions (including occasionally in a public service), but I do it only rarely. There are several reasons for my hesitancy.

First, if a person thoroughly understands the gospel, I see no reason why he cannot pray on his own to be saved. If he believes and understands the truth of the gospel, he should be able to express that truth verbally. Indeed, if he cannot express faith in Christ without my feeding him words, I am concerned that he hasn't truly understood the gospel.

Second, because works-based salvation is so embedded into our natural thought processes, I believe there is always a danger that by asking a person to repeat a prayer after me, they will (even subconsciously) be placing their faith in a "magical prayer"—no matter how many times I may tell them "it's not the exact words."

Third, asking a person to pray in his own words helps me understand how thoroughly he understood the gospel. Some people accuse fervent soulwinners who see people saved after the first presentation of the gospel as presenting a shallow message and harvesting premature fruit. They use accusatory terms such as "easy believism" or "1-2-3 pray after me." Are there soulwinners who present a gospel that is void of conviction of sin? Absolutely. Does the fact that a person responds to the gospel the first time he hears it clearly presented mean he has fallen to "easy believism"? Absolutely not. Many people in the New Testament responded to the gospel the first time they heard its simple message preached. But I don't see that those who were saved in the New Testament repeated a prayer after a soulwinner either. Of course, it's possible that they did, but it's not recorded, and I believe that inviting a person to pray to confess Christ as Saviour in his own words helps guard against false conversions.

Finally, when a person prays in his own words, it will solidify the decision he is making in his own mind and heart. His assurance will be anchored in Christ, rather than in the prayer I asked him to repeat after me.

I'm aware that some soulwinners have reasons they believe are equally as valid as mine for why they *do* invite a person to pray after them. I'm thankful for any person saved, and I recognize the validity of their arguments. As I mentioned before, I have myself on rare occasions done the same. I simply present the reasons above as a strong preference and as something to consider.

Preferences aside, there is one more key thought on presenting the gospel: we must do it. That is to say, you and I must be regularly sharing the gospel with the lost. Knowing the gospel and having expert ability to share its truth with others does no good if we don't actually do it.

THE GIFT AND ITS WRAPPING

When my wife wraps gifts for our children or grandchildren, she takes care in the wrapping she selects, even going so far as to consider the personality and interests of that particular child or grandchild. It is important to Terrie that the wrapping set a tone for the most important thing—the gift inside.

Similarly, when we present the gospel, we want to "wrap" it well. We want to use vocabulary our listeners can easily understand. We want to be clear and thorough in how we present it. But we never want to so focus on the wrapping that we overpower the gift.

Let me explain it this way: When you first become a Christian or when you first begin serving in gospel ministry, you have one overriding desire—to share the gospel—the gift of God—with others. It doesn't matter to you how the gift is packaged—what venue you have to share it. You just want everyone you know—and even those you don't know—to have the opportunity to receive Jesus Christ.

As times goes on, however, a subtle shift easily takes place. When you once focused on Jesus Himself—the Gift, you tend to focus more and more on how you package the gift—your presentation of the gospel, the specific programs of your church for outreach, or the actions of ministry.

This distraction is common to all of us. But in following this progression, we lose our passion for and focus on Jesus. Like small children at Christmas, we become enamoured with packaging while neglecting the gift itself.

As you seek to share the gospel with others, always remember two truths: First, to personally stay in love with Christ—to maintain a fervency and focus in your own walk with Him. When Jesus is your first love, the warmth of that love will bleed through your presentation of the gospel. Similarly, when your love for Christ has dulled through distraction, your gospel presentations will be empty of the fervency that comes through personal experience. They will become mere sales pitches, rather than "eyewitness" accounts of a personal disciple.

The second truth to remember is the simplicity of the gospel. The gospel is not a program. It's not a specific church ministry. It's not a chart or a list or a set of bullet points. It is a message of the death, burial, and resurrection of Christ for our sins. Don't lose the focus of the gospel: "the gift of God is eternal life through Jesus Christ our Lord."

ENTRUSTED WITH THE GOSPEL

Literally, the gospel is a trust. We have been commissioned, as representatives of Christ Himself, to present this vital message to people who are lost.

> *But as we were allowed of God to be put in trust with the gospel, even so we speak; not as pleasing men, but God, which trieth our hearts.*—1 THESSALONIANS 2:4

To wit, that God was in Christ, reconciling the world unto himself, not imputing their trespasses unto them; and hath committed unto us the word of reconciliation.
—2 CORINTHIANS 5:19

Being entrusted as an ambassador with the greatest message in the world is a privilege! We have everything we need—the message and the command. All that remains for us is to deliver the message. Who can you share the message with today?

NINE

THE RELATIONSHIPS OF A SOULWINNER

My grandmother Chappell first came in contact with the gospel through a soulwinner who went door-to-door, actually farm-to-farm, in the rural area of southwest Colorado where my grandparents were bean farmers. Pop Kinney, as he was called, wasn't turned off by my unsaved grandfather's hardness toward the gospel. Over the course of a summer, he worked to develop a relationship with Granddad, eventually resulting in both Granddad's and Grandmother's salvation.[1]

Granddad has been in Heaven for several years now, but Grandmother continues to be one of the most faithful and fruitful soulwinners I know. At ninety-five years old, she has arthritis and struggles to get around with a walker, so she can't get out as much as she used to. But that doesn't stop her from sharing the gospel! She practices a sort of "reverse doorknocking." Anyone who knocks on Grandmother's door—or crosses her path in any way—is going to hear the gospel. Neighbors, doctors (and she has a lot of them these days), her hair dresser, salesmen—they're not leaving her presence without an opportunity to hear the gospel.

Several weeks ago, Terrie and I were able to visit the family farm in Colorado. As we visited with Grandmother, she told us about Megan, one of the Visiting Angels who provides home health care for her. (Grandmother is fiercely independent and still lives alone.) She told of how kind and helpful Megan is, and (I knew even as she began the story that this part was coming soon) how on Megan's second visit she asked her if she knew the Lord. Megan didn't, so Grandmother shared the gospel with her…and Megan trusted Christ.

I remember at my grandmother's ninetieth birthday celebration a man standing and telling about coming to Grandmother's home in 1957. After a meal one evening, she took him (a young teenager at the time) into the living room, opened the Bible, and shared with him how he could become a Christian. As this man, Mr. Brown, shared this testimony, he began to weep and said it was the greatest day of his life and that since then his life has never been the same. After his testimony, others around the room also shared that it had been my grandmother who introduced them to Christ.

Grandmother understands a truth that many soulwinners neglect—every relationship in our lives should be stewarded for sharing the message of the gospel. Some Christians treat soulwinning as if God only saves people during a two-hour weekly time slot, and even then only after someone knocks on their door with a gospel invitation. Some Christians seem to further assume that people only get saved if they do so in their brief encounter with the soulwinner on their doorstep.

The truth is that relationships are as necessary to the spread of the gospel as any form of evangelism. Any relationship that God has placed in your life—family, friends, acquaintances, neighbors, classmates, coworkers—is an opportunity to share the gospel. And any soulwinning encounter that you can develop into a cultivated relationship for the purpose of sharing the gospel later is a vital opportunity as well. In this chapter, I'd like to share with you the necessity of cultivating relationships and a simple tool that I believe every soulwinner should use to aid them in this process.

BACKSTORY TO PENTECOST

Acts 2:41 records, "Then they that gladly received his word were baptized: and the same day there were added unto them about three thousand souls." It was the Apostle Peter whom God used to preach the gospel at Pentecost when three thousand people trusted Christ.

But do you remember who led Peter to Christ? It was his brother Andrew. John 1:41 says of Andrew, "He first findeth his own brother Simon, and saith unto him, We have found the Messias, which is, being interpreted, the Christ." I'm thankful that when Andrew realized he had found Christ he immediately told his brother! Andrew's faithfulness to witness to his own family played a part in the backstory to Pentecost—even though Andrew himself didn't preach the powerful sermon of Pentecost.

When you and I steward the relationships God has given us, who knows the outcomes of that faithfulness. Conversely, when we neglect relationships—the ones we've already been given or the ones we could develop—we neglect one of the most vital aspects of being a soulwinner.

PROSPECTS AND PROSPECT LISTS

John and Sue Johnson first visited Lancaster Baptist Church at the invitation of a coworker. By the time they arrived at church and got their two boys settled into the kids classes, they were a few minutes late to the service. As chance would have it, there were a couple of open seats right in the front—on the third row. An usher led them to the front and seated them there.

John was overcome by the choir special—especially by the Christian joy he saw on the faces of the choir members. He knew they had something he didn't have. As he then listened to the message, John was deeply convicted. He tells how he clung to his bulletin and could hardly look up at me. It seemed that every time he did, I was looking at him, and he was sure I was preaching directly to him. During the invitation, he clung to the seat in front of him with one desire—get out as quickly as possible. I wasn't preaching only to John, but I did notice the conviction written across his face, and I knew I needed to go by the Johnsons' house to share the gospel with them personally.

Much to John's dismay, Sue had filled out the guest card in the bulletin, giving our church office their address. The Tuesday evening following the Johnsons' visit, I stopped by their house.

They weren't home, so I left a note on the door: "Sorry I missed you, Pastor Chappell."

It turns out that the Johnsons were at a baseball game that evening for their sons, Paul and Ryan. They didn't find my note until Wednesday morning, and when they did, John was displeased. He wasn't really sure why he had even agreed to go to church the first time—curiosity, he supposed. But he didn't want more, and he didn't want the pastor to come and visit him. If only Sue hadn't given the church their address!

What John didn't know was that I had added him and Sue to my personal "prospect list." On this list, which I have maintained for many years, I collect names and addresses of people I have met or visited who have shown an interest in visiting church or in hearing the gospel. Once I add someone to this list, I do my best to consistently cultivate a relationship with them. I strive to call, visit, or write every person on my prospect list at least once a week. Once I've added someone to my list, they don't come off very easily—especially not just because they're not home the first time I visit!

The following Saturday morning, I stopped by again. Once again, the Johnsons were not home, and once again, I left a note. When John found the note Sunday afternoon (he had not gone to church Sunday morning), he was furious.

The following Tuesday morning, John was sitting in his office when a thought suddenly occurred to him. He recollected that the coworker who had first invited him to church had also once mentioned that the church had visitation on Tuesday nights and Saturday mornings. The visits of the previous week confirmed in his mind that this was indeed true. Now he knew when to anticipate my next visit. He picked up the phone and called Sue.

"Sue, the pastor is going to come by again tonight. I want you to dust off the big family Bible in the living room."

"What? You don't know that he's going to come."

"I do too."

"You can't know that."

An argument followed in which Sue expressed that she didn't appreciate being told how and what to clean. It ended with one of them hanging up on the other.

Thirty minutes later, however, John's office phone rang. It was Sue.

"John, you were right. They're coming tonight."

"Of course I'm right. But how do you know?"

"They called and set up an appointment. I told them they could come at 7:00 tonight."

Now it was John's turn to be frustrated. He still didn't like the idea of the visits, and he sure didn't like that Sue had told me that they'd be home. "Well, they can come see you, but I won't be home tonight."

As the day wore on, John softened, and, in mercy to Sue, he said he would come home to help her "handle those people." By the time I arrived at the Johnson residence at 7:00, the family Bible was dusted, and Paul and Ryan had been banished to their upstairs bedroom to play Nintendo and give us the living room to talk.

We sat in the living room where I opened God's Word and shared the wonderful message of salvation. John had many questions, and we talked for over two hours. Finally, about 9:15

that evening, John and Sue both bowed their heads and trusted Christ as their Saviour. Paul and Ryan, who had been stealthily listening from upstairs, just outside our line of sight, also trusted Christ within the next few weeks.

The transformation in John and Sue's life was immediate and thrilling. They soaked up God's Word like sponges, and they couldn't get enough preaching. We had a week-long prophecy conference soon after, and John loved having church every night. He asked me later if we could continue the nightly services every week.

That was twenty-two years ago. Today, John and Sue are still faithful members of Lancaster Baptist Church. They still come to every service and to special events. Both of their sons are also faithfully serving Christ. Paul and his wife are active in the children's ministry of their church in Virginia. Ryan graduated from West Coast Baptist College and married another WCBC graduate, who also happened to be the daughter of his Sunday school teacher. He now serves as the pastor of Redwood Baptist Church in Redwood City, California.

The Johnson family's salvation is to the glory of God! But I don't know that it would have happened without the coworker who stewarded her relationship to invite John to church in the first place. And I doubt John and Sue would have gotten saved without my using the tool of a prospect list to continue to follow up on them. What if I had made the first visit, found them not home, and never returned? What if I had neglected this contact that God entrusted to our church?

The Johnsons are not the only members of Lancaster Baptist Church who are there because of a prospect list. Scores of people in our church today were once on my or another soulwinner's prospect list. I've seen the Lord bless this simple tool and the diligence behind it over and over again.

NUTS AND BOLTS

Like any tool, the prospect list requires a slight learning curve. Most of that learning is simply a matter of remembering to use the list and then exercising diligence in keeping it updated. Listed below are some of the common questions soulwinners have regarding how to use this vital tool.

WHAT IS A PROSPECT LIST?

The prospect list is the single most important and effective soulwinning tool for stewarding gospel contacts.

Some people will trust Christ the very first time you share the gospel with them—even if it is the first time they met you. Others, however, will not. But that does not mean these others wouldn't trust Christ the second or third time you come by. Keeping and maintaining a prospect list allows you to be intentional and persistent in your efforts to develop a relationship and to share the gospel.

This list helps me follow up on people I've met out door knocking as well as seeing new Christians baptized, added to the church, and grounded through discipleship.

The prospect list is not complicated. It is a simple list of names with contact information and a record of attempts you've made to make contact. On the next page is a sample of the form commonly used among our church family:

FRIENDS&
ACQUAINTANCES
WHO NEED CHRIST

"…as my Father hath sent me, even so send I you."—John 20:21

FRIEND/ACQUAINTANCE

DATE OF FIRST CONTACT: ____ / ____ / ____

NAME

ADDRESS

CITY   ZIP

PHONE

POINT OF CONTACT

COMMENTS

CALLS

NOTES

VISITS

SAVED: ____ / ____ / ____   BAPTIZED: ____ / ____ / ____

sample prospect list

WHO DO I INCLUDE ON MY PROSPECT LIST?

You should add anyone you believe to be a positive contact for the gospel. This may be a guest who you met at church but is not saved (or not yet added to the church). It may be a coworker or classmate. It may be a business contact—a vendor or a client. It may be someone you met while you were soulwinning.

Some soulwinners approach door-to-door witnessing with a canvassing mentality. They knock doors on a particular street, and the brief encounter they have at each door is the only encounter until months or years later when they come to that street again.

I prefer to approach doorknocking with a shepherding mentality. I'll do my best at each door to gain an opportunity to share the gospel, but if the person is having dinner or it is a bad time for them to listen, I will ask if I can come back later. Similarly, if a person is receptive to my visit and perhaps even listens to the gospel but doesn't trust Christ, I want to develop a relationship with that person. It may be easier to knock only on fresh doors every time you go out soulwinning, but in so doing, you'll neglect people whose hearts the Holy Spirit began stirring by your first visit!

Another scenario may be if a person does allow me to share the gospel and trusts Christ. I don't want to leave this young Christian with a simple admonition to come to church. I'm going to keep following up on him until he is baptized and added to the church. In any of these cases, I'll give the contact my phone number and ask for his. I'll also jot down his address. All of this information I'll add to my prospect list immediately after soulwinning.

HOW DO I USE MY PROSPECT LIST?

Once you have a prospect list, what do you do with the names on it?

1. Pray daily—You can visit, call, and write notes, but only God can work in hearts. Use your prospect list as a daily prayer list, and it becomes ten times more valuable than it is as a simple contact list.

2. Contact weekly—I strive to contact each person on my prospect list at least once per week with either a visit, note, a phone call, or text. In some cases (as with the Johnsons) I will make multiple efforts toward contact in a given week if I don't actually connect with them on the first try. The key here is to diligently pursue them, not to simply ease my mind that I tried. Be sensitive, too, to the Holy Spirit in your efforts. There may be occasions to back off for a period of time or to send a note instead of making a visit. But whatever you do, don't neglect these contacts.

3. Update regularly—Your list is only as good as it is current. Be diligent in recording your weekly contacts, and periodically update your entire list. I'm very slow to remove someone from my prospect list, but there are occasions—such as when they have moved without giving me new contact information or they have expressed they are no longer interested—when I will remove a person from my list. Even still, if there is a chance that I may be able to renew contact with them later, I will keep their information and, as the Holy Spirit leads, reach out to them again, perhaps when we are having a special Sunday at church or it has been several weeks since I last tried.

CAN YOU HELP ME GET STARTED?

The form (showed on page 125) that soulwinners in our church family currently use is available for free download on the Striving Together website. You can access it by visiting the free resources section of www.strivingtogether.com.

Our church has also created an electronic prospect list available as a smart phone application. It is called Outreach Mobile and is available via iTunes and Android Play stores. This $0.99 app comes with a set of incredibly helpful features.

For each person you add to this electronic list, you can easily:

- View a map to their home
- Call by phone or send an email
- Record each contact and spiritual decision

And for each person, there are many available fields to record relevant information, such as the following:

- Date and place you first met
- Multiple phone numbers and contact information
- Names and ages of other members of the family
- Additional notes and info

CULTIVATING HEARTS FOR AN ABUNDANT HARVEST

Our job as soulwinners is to sow the gospel seed—faithfully and regularly. But, as stated previously, not everyone is saved the first time the seed is sown in his heart. In 1 Corinthians 3:6, the Apostle Paul wrote, "I have planted, Apollos watered; but God gave the increase." Jesus told His disciples in John 4:34, "I sent you to reap that whereon ye bestowed no labour: other men laboured, and ye are entered into their labours."

The soil of many hearts requires cultivating to produce a harvest. If, when we encounter hearts that need to be cultivated, we only race on to sow the gospel in more places, we'll neglect relationships God would use to produce spiritual fruit.

Fruitful soulwinners cultivate relationships. And every consistently fruitful soulwinner who I have known has consistently used some form of a prospect list (be it 3x5 cards or an electronic app) as a tool to cultivate these relationships.

Who do you already have a relationship with who needs the gospel? Perhaps a neighbor, a coworker, a business acquaintance. Look for an opportunity to share the gospel with them. Who knows? God may use you as an "Andrew" to lead a "Peter" to Christ who will lead thousands more to the Lord!

Who have you recently spoken with about the Lord who needs you to go back? Do you hope to soon meet someone who may be nearly ready to be saved? What system do you have in place to track your efforts in cultivating a relationship with them?

I challenge you to take a specific step of action before the end of today: begin a prospect list. You can use the resources suggested in this chapter. You can even use a stack of 3x5 cards hole-punched and placed in a metal ring. But whatever you use, use something!

If you are a soulwinning Christian with a heart for God and a responsiveness to the promptings of the Holy Spirit, you will have people who need you to cultivate their hearts through a relationship. A prospect list is the single best tool I know to use to steward the contacts God gives me for the gospel.

And if you would like more contacts, read on to the next chapter!

---

1   For the full story of Pop Kinney, my grandparents' salvation, and the resulting fruit, see chapter 14 in *Stewarding Life* (Striving Together Publications, 2011).

T E N

THE FAITH
OF A SOULWINNER

For Rostam[1] to gain an approved visa to come to the United States from Iran was a miracle in itself. That his wife, Goli, and her sister, Souri, were also able to come around the same time was a greater miracle.

But Rostam had no inkling of the surprise he was in for. Within days of setting foot on American soil and being welcomed into Goli's uncle's house, Goli's tenth-grade cousin, Anthony, invited Rostam and Goli to church.

Two weeks previous, Anthony had received an invitation to the annual Christmas musical at Lancaster Baptist Church. He really wanted to attend, and his mom agreed to take him. Anthony loved it, and he asked his mom to take him again the following Sunday. Souri (who arrived in the States ahead of Rostam and Goli) attended as well. In teen Sunday school that day, Anthony trusted Christ as his Saviour. The following Tuesday, Anthony's Sunday school teacher visited Anthony at his home and shared the gospel with Souri who put her faith in Christ that evening.

When Anthony invited Rostam and Goli to come to church with him, they agreed—more out of curiosity than anything. Living in a country where Islam is the state religion, they had never experienced other religions.

Rostam listened carefully to the preaching. He had never heard that God loved him, that God had come in the flesh to pay for his sins, or that he could have his sins completely forgiven. Rostam attended the next Sunday. And the next.

By this time, a teacher of one of our adult Sunday school classes had invited Rostam and Goli to attend class. They did, and after class the teacher shared the gospel with them again. Both confirmed that they did indeed want to place their faith in Christ. They trusted Christ that morning and asked to be baptized in the Sunday evening service.

After Rostam was saved, his spiritual appetite was insatiable. He devoured God's Word, although he had to read it in a language that was still new to him. He listened attentively to preaching. And when he was invited to begin formal discipleship with one of our associate pastors, he jumped at the chance, asking to meet more than once per week. In fact, he asked for permission to translate the discipleship material into his own language, an undertaking which he has already completed.

Early on in his spiritual growth, Rostam expressed to me his desire to return to Iran—not as a career man (although he has both bachelor's and master's degrees in respected fields), but as a church planter. Recently, he did return to Iran with a well-thought-out written strategy for reaching his people with the gospel. Pray for Rostam and his wife as, in a hostile Muslim country, they share the gospel of Christ.

GOOD SOIL, REAL FAITH

We know that Christ has called us to go into all the world and preach the gospel. We've seen the command in black and white.

We also know from Christ's parable of the sower and the seed[2] that there are various types of hearts we encounter as we plant the seed of the gospel. Some hearts—like some types of soil—are hard; some are thorny; some are stony; and some are tender. Our job is to faithfully sow the seed into *all* hearts because only God knows who is ready to hear it. Those with hearts already prepared by the work of the Holy Spirit will respond.

But to listen to the average Christian today, you would think that *all* hearts are hard or stony. We have developed layers of excuses for why we don't believe people will respond to the gospel. Our excuses, of course, have an element of truth. Some people won't respond.

But I'm here to tell you that there are *millions* of people today who truly want to know the power of the forgiveness of Jesus Christ.

In the end, our willingness to obey the Great Commission is directly tied to our faith in God's power. If I believe that no one wants to hear or respond to the gospel, I won't share it. And if I don't share it, no one will respond.

If, however, I believe that God has entrusted me with His truth and commanded me to share it, and that He has prepared hearts to receive His truth—if I am faith-filled—I will be faithful in my obedience.

From a human standpoint, Rostam, Goli, and Souri would be three of the least likely people to hear the gospel and trust Christ—especially after hearing it fewer than five times. Yet, each of these had hearts that were good ground. God had prepared their hearts, and when they heard of a loving God who had already provided forgiveness and eternal life, they responded.

But what if our church had not been sowing the seed? What if no one had invited Anthony to the Christmas musical? What if Anthony's Sunday school teacher had assumed he wasn't interested in spiritual things? What if he hadn't asked Anthony to stay after class and thoroughly explained salvation to him?

What if Anthony had assumed his cousins would never convert from Islam? What if he had never invited them to church? What if I had not preached the plain gospel message those three Sundays when they attended before their salvation? What if the teacher had not invited them to his class? What if he had not personally explained the gospel to them? What if he had assumed they needed to hear it more times and had not invited them to make a decision?

It takes faith to engage in the Great Commission. And I'm concerned that in the hearts of too many Christians our faith is waning.

WHERE FAITH AND COURAGE MEET

His name is Danut Gavra—Dan to us Americans. I met him last winter while preaching a conference in Timisoara, Romania. Even before we talked, his missing leg told me that he had a story. The missionary I was with knew the story and asked him to share it with me.

Dan was twenty-four years old in 1989. On Friday morning, December 15, he arrived in the town square of Timisoara on the public transportation bus after a long night of work. He saw a crowd gathering outside the home of Pastor Laszlo Tokes, the pastor of one of the churches in Timisoara.

Pastor Tokes had been a source of concern to the Communists for some time. He had been speaking against their oppression of religion in his sermons, and rumors were spreading. Dan feared the worst as he hurried over to the gathering crowd.

In hushed whispers people shared with each other what they had heard on their radios through contrabanded stations: Pastor Tokes was being "transitioned" to another church in the country. In reality, the crowd knew this was not a voluntary transition, nor would it be a kind one. Many from his church showed up at the church steps to block the officers' way. By the time Dan arrived, others were gathering as well—including Dan's pastor and his son.

Throughout the day, more people joined the ranks of those on the street until eventually the entire town had gathered.

The Communists had first thought they could outwait the crowd, but as evening approached, they saw they were wrong.

The mayor appeared and urged people to leave, insisting there was no need to stay and the pastor would not be moved. Plain clothes security officers spread throughout the crowd echoed the similar stories.

But Dan didn't believe them.

As darkness fell, people wanted to believe the story. In small groups, they began to disperse toward their homes. Dan watched with growing concern.

With a flash of courageous inspiration, Dan made his way out of the crowd to a nearby orthodox church where he knew he could find candles. He purchased as many as he could carry and returned to the town square ten minutes later.

There on the square, Dan lit the first candle. Others crowded in, and he handed out the other candles he had purchased, lighting each from his. When Dan's candle supply ran out, he asked people to break their candles in half and share with each other.

All night, they kept the vigil with their lights.

It started with one small flame, but Dan had no way to know how brightly it would soon burn.

On Saturday morning, Dan had to leave for a family obligation in another village, but he later learned that the protest that began as a watch over one pastor's religious freedom turned into a protest for complete freedom.

Townspeople began calling, "Down with Communism!" "Freedom for Romania!"

Violence soon ensued as the Communists retaliated. They broke into Pastor Tokes' church, beat him and his wife, and dragged them off. The town quieted, but the protest continued, albeit at a lower key.

Dan returned to town Sunday morning to attend church. That afternoon, the townspeople escalated their protest once again. In large groups, they marched on the Communist Headquarters in the City Hall. They ripped and burned pictures of President Nicolae Ceausescu.

As dusk began to fall, Dan gathered a group of a few hundred students to go to the headquarters of the militia police station and demand release of the prisoners the Communists had taken during the protest. By the time the group approached a bridge they must pass, it was dark. Unfortunately, the darkness hid the sinister figures ahead—the army was waiting for them on the bridge.

As machine gun bullets whistled through the air, the young woman next to Dan fell. By the time Dan realized she had been shot and was dead, his left leg was shot out from under him—severed from his body.

Dan woke up in the hospital some hours later. Over the next five days, he listened carefully to the reports coming in until he heard on December 24—just nine days after he lit the first candle—that Ceausescu had been killed. Romania was free at last.

A few days after Christmas, Dan's pastor came to see him in the hospital. When he expressed sorrow over the loss of Dan's leg, Dan answered, "I don't mind so much the loss of my leg. After all, it was I who lit the first candle."

WHERE IS OUR FAITH?

I believe many of us approach the Great Commission with unbelief. We don't actually believe it can be done.

We've adapted a "wait and see" attitude when it comes to evangelism. We'll put out a little effort here and there, but we want to be assured of success before we truly invest ourselves.

But here's the thing about doing something great for God: you do it in faith. That is how it has always been, and soulwinners who don't act in faith don't get to see the blessings of obedience.

We look at the Great Commission somewhat like a peasant would look at an assignment to overthrow a Communist leader. Beyond unlikely—impossible.

Or is it?

It wasn't for Dan.

But he never would have known if he hadn't lit the first candle.

If we are to fully engage in the Great Commission, we need the faith and courage of men like Dan. We need to shed our "wait and see" attitudes—insistent on seeing success before we invest ourselves—and develop "I'm all in" attitudes.

Did Christ give us a command He cannot enable us to obey? No. But when we choose to believe He did, we fail to obey.

The results belong to God, but obedience belongs to us.

If we are to obey fully the Great Commission, we need faith. Faith to do the hard work—to regularly, persistently share the gospel. Faith to believe it can be done. Faith to invest the obedience required to make it happen.

Where are the Christians with the faith, passion, and courage to say, "It can be done, and with God's help, I'm going to make it happen"?

STRATEGY FOR SUCCESS

Our best strategy in reaching the world with the gospel is contained in one word: obedience.

We can brainstorm and innovate; we can read—or write—books on soulwinning; but until we put on our shoes and walk across the street to witness to a lost person, we haven't truly engaged.

Do you want to see God use you to reach people with the gospel? Your best strategy—your only strategy—is faith-filled obedience to Christ's command.

Are you willing to obey in faith? If so, forge ahead to Part 3 for specific ways you can engage in the Great Commission through your local church.

---

1   The names throughout this book are real. I have, however, changed Rostam's name as well as the names of his wife and sister-in-law for security reasons.

2   Matthew 13:3–23; Mark 4:3–20; Luke 8:5–15.

PART THREE

ENGAGING AS LOCAL CHURCHES

ELEVEN

THE ROLE OF THE LOCAL CHURCH IN SOULWINNING

Every church has a story. It is written, as all of our stories are, by the pen of history—a chronology of the events as they occur.

But the story of a church is more than history. It is shaped by the lives of the people who make up the church, and it is developed as the church reaches more people.

I'd like to give you a few glimpses into the story of our church by giving you snapshots of points when the gospel connected with the lives of people. These snapshots are of people who are part of our church today. Some have been reached recently, and some years ago. As you read, try to notice the common thread that pulls these stories together.

SNAPSHOT 1

Every couple of months, we organize a coffee and biscotti fellowship after the 11:00 morning service for those who are newer to our church. It was during one of these fellowships a few weeks ago that I met Warner and Carmen Chavez and their three sons.

It just so happened that this was the Chavezes' first Sunday to attend Lancaster Baptist. As we chatted, I sensed through the conversation that Carmen wasn't saved and had never clearly understood the gospel. I asked her if she knew the Lord as her personal Saviour. She did not, and she allowed me to share with her how she could know Him.

Right there at the side of the room we found chairs, and I opened God's Word to show Carmen God's simple plan of salvation. And right there, Carmen trusted Christ as her Saviour.

After we prayed, Carmen told me why they had come to church that day. "A couple of years ago, a man from this church came by my house and invited me to church. I didn't go then, but just last week, another man came by and talked to my husband. Warner prayed to get saved." Then the tears welled up in her eyes, "And now we're both saved."

I write this on a Monday—two weeks after the coffee and biscotti fellowship. Carmen and Warner and their three sons (who also trusted Christ that Sunday) were baptized yesterday. They have enrolled in one of the Sunday morning adult Bible classes of our church and are excited to begin their journey of faith.

SNAPSHOT 2

A few years ago, Mike and Mileny Halter shook my hand after a church service—their first service at Lancaster Baptist Church. The couple had been to other churches, although never regularly.

What impressed Mike was the gospel—he said he had never heard anything like that before. And he asked me if we could talk about it further sometime.

"Sometime" was that very afternoon in my office. About an hour later, Mike trusted Christ as his Saviour. He was baptized soon after. Mileny was already saved, and together, Mike and Mileny are serving the Lord and growing as young Christians.

SNAPSHOT 3

Kevin and Olga Rivero moved to the Antelope Valley by military appointment to the nearby Edwards Air Force Base. A man in our church led them to Christ in their home. They were soon baptized, and they began to grow in the Lord.

Soon after their salvation, however, the military moved them again. The couple found a Bible-preaching church and got plugged in.

Three years ago, Kevin and Olga moved back to Lancaster. They enrolled in our church's formal discipleship program for further grounding in their faith. Just a few weeks ago, Kevin greeted me after church. He couldn't have been more excited as he told me that he and Olga had just begun leading a new couple through discipleship.

SNAPSHOT 4

Josh Camarena trusted Christ early in life, but by the time he came to Lancaster Baptist with his girlfriend, Jordan, he had strayed far from the Lord. The Tuesday evening following their visit, one of the men in our church visited their home and led Jordan to Christ. Josh also made assurance of his salvation.

Right away, Josh and Jordan were faithful in their church attendance, but they had an obvious decision facing them—they needed to honor the Lord in their relationship with one another. With encouragement, counseling, and prayer, Josh and Jordan determined to get married. Shortly after their wedding, they presented themselves for baptism.

The couple has completed our discipleship program and is actively serving in church ministries. They recently brought two couples to church as their guests. A few days later, Josh asked another man in his class for coaching on how to lead someone to Christ. Josh and Jordan made the follow-up visits on their guests, and one of the couples trusted Christ as Saviour.

SNAPSHOT 5

Felix and Judy Dizon were behind one of the doors that two ladies in our church knocked on one Tuesday afternoon. The Dizons were new to the community and were excited to meet the ladies from our church. In fact, they told the ladies that they were looking for a church in their new community. Specifically, they were looking for a Father to come by and bless their home.

The soulwinners recognized the Dizons' obvious Filipino Catholic heritage. They knew that it was culturally based and that they didn't really understand what they believed (as they didn't see the difference between Baptists and Catholics). One of the ladies, Bonnie Ferrso, told the Dizons that her husband, Jerry, was one of the associate pastors at our church and would be happy to come pray with them over their new home. Before she left, she had Jerry scheduled for a home-blessing ceremony on the coming weekend.

Jerry was happy for a soulwinning opportunity, but he was unsure of what to do for a "home-blessing ceremony." As he approached the house he noticed cars were parked everywhere on the street. The Dizons had invited their family and friends over for the occasion. Felix formally introduced Jerry to the crowd: "Father Ferrso is here to bless our new home."

Jerry read from Psalm 127 and John 3 and briefly commented about both passages—first on the need of God's blessing over a family and second on the need for the new birth for each individual. Without pressing them for a decision regarding salvation, he prayed for the Dizon family. Before leaving, he asked the young couple if he could return to their home later to talk to them about church and the Lord. They happily agreed and set an appointment time.

The following Saturday, Jerry led both Felix and Judy to the Lord in their living room. Two weeks later, they followed Christ in baptism. Not long after, their two daughters were saved and baptized.

Today, the Dizon family are still members of Lancaster Baptist Church, and Felix and Judy are faithful soulwinners, regularly leading people to Christ. Their daughters are in Bible college, preparing to serve the Lord.

A COMPOSITE PICTURE

In many respects, these five snapshots are different. In each of these lives, there were unique situational dynamics that caused them to consider spiritual realities.

Yet, there is one factor that all five of these families have in common. From the Chavez family saved just two weeks ago to the Dizon family saved fifteen years ago, there is a common denominator that was instrumental in their salvation and has influenced and supported their spiritual growth like no other force could do.

It is the local church.

Consider the role the church played in all five of these testimonies.

The church provided an opportunity for soulwinners to connect in an organized effort to reach the community.

The church provided a place for these young Christians to be nurtured in the Lord.

The church provided opportunities for intentional discipleship. It provided encouragement, spiritually based relationships, and consistent instruction. It provided opportunities to hear the preaching of God's Word, accountability in growth, and clear teaching on practical, biblical steps of growth.

I believe this is why Christ delivered the Great Commission to the local church. The church is the "pillar and ground of the truth" (1 Timothy 3:15). It is the church that has at her disposal the resources to fulfill this commission—as a church.

And best of all, when you determine to obey Christ's command to engage in the Great Commission, you get to do so with the greatest organization on earth—the local New Testament church.

Conversely, to ignore the local church in your evangelism efforts is to ignore the very vehicle God designed to carry out Christ's mission. It's like driving to work but leaving your car behind—a ludicrous and costly mistake.

SPECIALLY EQUIPPED FOR A VITAL MISSION

When our nation sends military troops to the front lines, we don't send them without equipment. And we don't send them as individual soldiers either. We send them in units, and we provide them with training and supplies. In a similar way, Christ has specially equipped the local church for the "front lines" mission of reaching people with the gospel.

Over the years, there have been helpful non-profit ministries established that are not specifically local church ministries. Often called para-church ministries, these organizations have done tremendous good. They vary in purpose. Some exist to feed the homeless or provide education for children in third-world countries. Some are more evangelistic in nature and see many people reached for Christ annually. I'm thankful for every person reached for Christ through a para-church organization. But while these ministries do much good, they are not the vehicle commissioned by Christ with the Great Commission. In fact, they depend on local churches for support, help, and often for leadership as well.

Every Christian who is serious about the Great Commission needs to be part of a local church, for it is the church who has been charged and equipped by God to reach the world.

Consider four resources that Christ has distinctly built into the local church:

SPIRITUAL LEADERSHIP

And he gave some, apostles; and some, prophets; and some, evangelists; and some, pastors and teachers; For the perfecting of the saints, for the work of

> *the ministry, for the edifying of the body of Christ:*
> —Ephesians 4:11–12

From the conception of the local church, God has ordained for it to be led by godly, spiritual leaders.[1] The purpose for this leadership? To perfect (to mature) Christians for the work of the ministry and to edify (to build up) the body of Christ. With God's plan of leadership, the local church is equipped to train members to reach others with the gospel and to mature those new believers to be a vital part of the church's mission.

SPIRITUAL GIFTS

> *For as we have many members in one body, and all members have not the same office: So we, being many, are one body in Christ, and every one members one of another. Having then gifts differing according to the grace that is given to us, whether prophecy, let us prophesy according to the proportion of faith; Or ministry, let us wait on our ministering: or he that teacheth, on teaching; Or he that exhorteth, on exhortation: he that giveth, let him do it with simplicity; he that ruleth, with diligence; he that sheweth mercy, with cheerfulness.*
> —Romans 12:4–8

God gives every Christian spiritual gifts—divine enablement for ministry. Scripture likens these gifts to the parts of a body; individually, one part may be insignificant or incapable, but when functioning as a whole, each part is needed and sufficient. The context and the usefulness of these gifts is within the local church body.

SPIRITUAL PROCESSES

And the things that thou hast heard of me among many witnesses, the same commit thou to faithful men, who shall be able to teach others also.—2 TIMOTHY 2:2

Not forsaking the assembling of ourselves together, as the manner of some is; but exhorting one another: and so much the more, as ye see the day approaching.—HEBREWS 10:25

Within the blueprint of local church ministry is a structure that provides discipleship, accountability, and growth. God commands Christians to reproduce themselves through discipleship, and He instructs the church to develop spiritually edifying relationships of accountability and encouragement. A church that is obeying these commands has the structure to reach new people with the gospel, disciple new Christians, and lead Christians to biblical steps of growth.

SPIRITUAL STRATEGY

As they ministered to the Lord, and fasted, the Holy Ghost said, Separate me Barnabas and Saul for the work whereunto I have called them. And when they had ordained them elders in every church, and had prayed with fasting, they commended them to the Lord, on whom they believed. And so were the churches established in the faith, and increased in number daily.—ACTS 13:2, 14:23, 16:5

How did the gospel spread in the first century? By local churches planting local churches. In Acts 13 we see a clear picture of this process. A Great Commission-focused church was doing the work of the Lord when God called from her midst men to further the work in other places. Those missionaries planted churches in the cities to which they carried the gospel.

Churches planting churches is still God's plan today for the spread of the gospel. Individuals may have a vision to reach pockets of people, but it is the local church that is equipped to strategically preach the gospel to every creature (Mark 16:15).

ONWARD, FORWARD!

Some Christians see the local church as a personal resource. They consider what the church can do for them and for their families. They evaluate the church's ministries and leadership based on personal, social, or spiritual benefit they receive.

However, Christ didn't create the church to be a personal resource. He established it to be a present gospel force. He commanded us to take the gospel to every creature, and in the local church He gave us the resources to do it.

In John F. Kennedy's inaugural address, he made the famous statement, "Ask not what your country can do for you; ask what you can do for your country."[2] Similarly, I challenge you, "Ask not what your church can do for you; ask what you can do through your church to obey the Great Commission of Christ."

Too many Christians think of the local church as a luxury vehicle—equipped to meet their needs. Think instead of the local church as a utility vehicle—equipped to reach the world with the gospel of Jesus Christ.

If you are a pastor, I challenge you to prayerfully and strategically direct your church in obeying the Great Commission—in your own community and through church planting missionaries around the world. If you are not a pastor, I challenge you to invest yourself in your church's efforts of witnessing for Christ and nurturing new Christians in the faith.

In our next chapter, we'll more closely examine how a local church can organize its soulwinning program to saturate its community with the gospel. And we'll see how you can be engaged in helping your church to press forward in reaching the lost.

---

1   First Timothy 3 and Titus 1 detail the biblical qualifications for these leaders.

2   Suzanne McIntire and William E. Burns, *Speeches in World History* (Infobase Publishing, 2009), 450.

TWELVE

THE SOULWINNING PROGRAM OF THE LOCAL CHURCH

Do you dream of doing something great for God? I do! I dream of reaching our community with the gospel of Jesus Christ. I dream of seeing more people come to Christ through the soulwinning ministries of our church this year than last year. I dream of seeing more lives changed and families transformed by the power of the gospel. I dream of watching more young Christians—passionate about their faith and growing in their daily walk—begin to lead others to Christ. In short, I dream of what happens when a local church corporately obeys the Great Commission of Christ!

I hope you dream for this as well. I hope as you've read these chapters your desire to see the Great Commission carried out through your local church—through your personal obedience—has grown. I hope you dream of increased fruit—multiplied fruit.

But here's the thing about a dream—it only works if you do. After all, a dream without a plan is only a wish.

So let's look again at our dream. If you and I long to see our communities reached with the gospel of Christ by our obedience to the Great Commission, we must have a plan for how to see this dream realized. And if we desire for the fruit of our dream to be lasting, our plan must be thoroughly biblical and empowered by the Holy Spirit.

In this chapter, I would like to share with you such a plan—a local church strategy for organizing the efforts of the church to reach the lost within our communities. Whether you are a pastor desiring to better organize the soulwinning efforts of your church, a leader in the church helping the pastor, or a soulwinner wanting to understand how you can better sync your soulwinning with the outreach of your church, I pray this chapter will give you helpful, practical advice.

So how do we do it? How do we organize the local church to reach the people in our communities?

CLARIFYING THE DREAM

It's one thing to state a general dream; it's another thing to put that dream into a clear purpose statement. When we say we want to "reach our community with the gospel," what do we mean? What is our purpose?

Biblically, our purpose is three fold:

1. To win the lost. We believe that in our communities there are still people who need the gospel. We believe there are still men, women, boys, and girls who would respond to the

Word of God if a Spirit-filled soulwinner would present God's gracious offer of salvation to them. Furthermore, we desire to *be* those soulwinners who witness for Christ and see lost people trust Christ.

2. To saturate the community with the gospel. Paul wrote to the church at Thessalonica, "For from you sounded out the word of the Lord not only in Macedonia and Achaia, but also in every place your faith to God-ward is spread abroad; so that we need not to speak any thing" (1 Thessalonians 1:8). This church had so effectively witnessed for Christ that they had not only saturated their own community with the gospel, but they had witnessed to those who merely passed through their community on the famous Egnatian Way, thus sending the gospel into regions far beyond Thessalonica.

We are commanded to take the gospel into *all* the world. This includes our own communities as well as every other nation on the globe. Fully accomplishing this task is only possible through a biblical missions strategy.[1] (To take the gospel to Africa, we need to support missionaries who will go to Africa.) But accomplishing this task in our *own* community requires a biblical saturation strategy. In this chapter, I will suggest a soulwinning strategy that enables your church to saturate your community thoroughly with the gospel of Christ—so the gospel is purposefully and systematically taken to every home and made available through every venue you can use.

3. To train Christians in witnessing for Christ. An effective church soulwinning program not only provides opportunities for members to go soulwinning, but it is structured to reproduce new soulwinners. Soulwinning is not the job of the pastor or the church staff; it is the job of every Christian. Philippians 1:27 instructs local churches to *strive together* "for the faith of the gospel." This isn't just a pastor and church staff endeavor. It is a *church* endeavor.

Ephesians 4:11–12 says, "And he gave some, apostles; and some, prophets; and some, evangelists; and some, pastors and teachers; For the perfecting of the saints, for the work of the ministry, for the edifying of the body of Christ." Ministry is not for a select few—the pastor and church staff. It is for the entire church. My job as a pastor is to equip the church to accomplish its mission, not for me as pastor to accomplish the mission alone.

Christ Himself gave us this pattern. True, He began His ministry alone, but He soon called out twelve apostles. He mentored and trained them, and He sent them to preach: "Then he called his twelve disciples together…And he sent them to preach the kingdom of God, and to heal the sick" (Luke 9:1–2).

But Christ didn't stop with the twelve. The following chapter records, "After these things the Lord appointed other seventy also, and sent them two and two before his face into every city and place, whither he himself would come" (Luke 10:1).

And just before He ascended to Heaven, Jesus commissioned—not just twelve, or seventy—but the local church to preach the gospel: "Go ye therefore, and teach all nations, baptizing them in the name of the Father, and of the Son, and of the Holy Ghost: Teaching them to observe all things whatsoever I have commanded you: and, lo, I am with you alway, even unto the end of the world. Amen" (Matthew 28:19–20).

One of the great by-products of an effective church soulwinning program is the reproduction of soulwinners. As someone wisely stated, "It is only as we develop others around us that we permanently succeed." But this developing others doesn't happen by accident. It must be woven into the fabric of the church soulwinning program. Although resources that teach Christians to share their faith abound today, there is still no substitute for an experienced soulwinner taking someone else under his wing and teaching him how to lead people to Christ!

HOW OTHERS CATCH THE VISION

The fact that you're reading this book—and have continued reading through Chapter 12—is a pretty good indication that you have a vision to grow as a soulwinner. I'm guessing, too, that you desire to see that vision increased in others as well. So how do you stir the enthusiasm of others?

There is a simple secret: soulwinning is better caught than taught. If you desire to encourage others in soulwinning—whether you are the pastor or a church member—you must be a personal soulwinner.

I believe the reason that the Apostle Paul was able to so faithfully and thoroughly raise up young leaders was he was a biblical example—he provided a model for them of godly living and faithful witnessing.

In Romans 1:15–16, Paul wrote, "So, as much as in me is, I am ready to preach the gospel to you that are at Rome also. For I am not ashamed of the gospel of Christ: for it is the power of God unto salvation to everyone that believeth; to the Jew first, and also to the Greek."

Paul didn't just *tell* others to win souls. He did it. This is the biblical model of raising up soulwinners. If you desire to see those around you catch a heart for soulwinning, if you desire to ignite (or reignite) soulwinning fervor in your church family, others need to sense that fervor from *you*.

Be present at the public soulwinning meetings. Share testimonies of people God has recently allowed you to lead to Christ through soulwinning. Invite others in your church to join you in doorknocking and making follow-up calls. Be diligent in your personal efforts to stay after winning souls.

If you've been a soulwinner in the past but are growing weary, I challenge you, press on! If you've never been earnest or diligent in personal soulwinning, I challenge you, begin now! Others in your church need your example and your enthusiasm.

CHURCH SIZE AND DREAM SIZE

If you come to a soulwinning meeting at Lancaster Baptist Church on an average Saturday morning, you'll find over forty baskets lining the walls around the auditorium where we meet. Each basket holds maps, prospect visits, and follow-up visits for a particular adult Bible class of our church. An easy false takeaway from this scene would be that Lancaster Baptist Church can be an effective soulwinning church because of its size. After all, with over forty adult Bible classes represented in a single morning of outreach, how could we not see new growth added to the church, right?

Before you read any further in this chapter, I want to dispel a popular myth—that the size of a church is proportionate to the ability of the church to be effective in soulwinning. Quite simply, you do not have to be a large church to be an effective soulwinning church.

How do I know? In part, I know because there are hundreds of churches around our nation that are not large—some are new church plants, some are churches in rural areas—and yet they have effective soulwinning programs.

Mostly, however, I know this from personal experience. When the Lord brought our family to Lancaster, the church had fewer than twenty people. There was no soulwinning program when we came—there were no programs of *any* kind! I remember when I had the first gospel tracts for the church printed and I asked the printer to include phrases like, "Exciting children's program, active youth group, and vibrant music." The "exciting children's program" was run by my wife who taught nursery through sixth grade each Sunday morning. The "vibrant music" consisted of my opening the hymnal and leading congregational singing—with no piano. The "active youth group" was purely visionary—we actually only had one teenager!

So when I say that a church doesn't have to be large to be an effective soulwinning church, I know what I'm talking about. The soulwinning program at Lancaster Baptist began with my daily knocking on doors—at least five hundred per week—asking people if they knew if they were going to Heaven. I invited men in our church to join me on Tuesday evenings and Saturday mornings, and those invitations were the seeds of our soulwinning program. God blessed our early efforts, and pretty soon newly saved Christians were added to the church.

Later, as we grew and added more adult Sunday school classes, we began organizing the soulwinning program through these classes. The forty soulwinning baskets you may see at our church today were once a stack of 3x5 cards on my desk. Yet even when we had only a handful of people to go soulwinning, we had an effective soulwinning ministry. Most of the people in our church—longtime members and brand-new Christians—have been led to Christ through the soulwinning and outreach ministries of our church family.

As I look back over the past twenty-eight years of ministry here in Lancaster, I can confidently say that the size of our church has never been the determining factor of the effectiveness of our soulwinning. In fact, as we have grown, we have had to purposefully strive to keep soulwinning our main focus. Soulwinning effectiveness is in no way tied to church size. It has always been and always will be related to individual Christians being filled with the Spirit, trained in sharing the gospel, and equipped through a well-organized soulwinning program. God blesses obedience, not size.

A STRATEGY OVERVIEW

So what about a specific strategy for reaching your community with the gospel? How can you systematically saturate your community? And what can you—as a pastor or as a church member—do to provide structure and/or support?

I suggest a four-word strategy for organizing the soulwinning efforts within the local church. I'll expand on each word in a moment, but here is a brief overview:

Times—You need scheduled soulwinning times to coordinate the efforts of multiple soulwinners. Some people will go soulwinning at different times as they have opportunity, but scheduling soulwinning meetings overcomes one of the biggest hurdles of many well-meaning Christians—no time. What gets scheduled gets done, and scheduling all-church soulwinning opportunities helps individuals add soulwinning to their individual schedules!

Supplies—At these soulwinning meetings, there should be supplies available for those who go out—tracts, maps of areas to knock on doors, and prepared visits.

Instruction—New soulwinners need instruction in presenting the gospel, and experienced soulwinners appreciate advanced training in sharing their faith.

Program—From systematically knocking on every door in your community to thoroughly following up on prospects and guests, you need a predetermined program.

So there it is—times, supplies, instruction, and program. In every aspect of this plan there are many opportunities for any member of the church to jump in and help. From making sure there are tracts available, to highlighting maps (explained below), to entering visitor information in a database—there are 101 ways that you can help. And if you are overseeing these areas, there are 101 ways that you can involve others in serving.

Before we look at each of these areas in more detail, I want to give a word of advice concerning general organization of the soulwinning program.

TO THE PASTOR OR LEADER OVERSEEING THE SOULWINNING PROGRAM

As you provide oversight in the soulwinning program of the church, there are two suggestions, by way of experience, that I would make.

The first concerns an annual "soulwinning kickoff." We hold this every fall at Lancaster Baptist Church. (The name was originally derived because it coincides with the beginning of football season. In the early years, we themed the "kickoff service" around football.) The purpose of the soulwinning kickoff is to enlist new soulwinners and solidify the commitment (or reenlistment) of seasoned soulwinners. This is one of the largest events on our annual calendar, rivaled only by our annual fall outreach Sunday about six weeks later. (We purposefully time this kickoff to precede the most intense season of outreach on our church calendar.)

The soulwinning kickoff consists of a soulwinning-themed church service with a message specifically addressing our responsibility to obey the Great Commission through personal soulwinning. For many years, we held this service on a Wednesday evening. In recent years, I've moved this message to a Sunday morning—with less football theming!

The soulwinning kickoff is vital for two reasons: It reinforces that our commission as a church is to give the gospel to our community, and it gives each member of our church an opportunity to commit to engage in this commission.

The second suggestion is to organize the soulwinning program through the adult Bible classes of the church. As I mentioned above, we have done this for many years now. For a couple of Sundays before the kickoff service (and often the Sunday following as well), we provide cards (see sample below) in each adult Bible class for soulwinners to sign up for the new season of soulwinning. Each card provides options for soulwinners to note which adult class they attend, what time of week they will go soulwinning, and their level of experience.

RENEW
Fall Soulwinning Kickoff

Name: (please print)_____

Adult Bible Fellowship: _____

Email Address: _____

I plan to go soulwinning at the following time: (choose one)

☐ Wednesday mornings   9:30 AM   North Auditorium
☐ Wednesday evenings   6:30 PM   North Auditorium
☐ Wednesday evenings   6:30 PM   West Palmdale Residence
☐ Saturday mornings   10:00 AM   North Auditorium

Enroll me in:

☐ Netcasters elective, 4-week class to sharpen my witness, beginning 9/4
☐ Renew Soulwinning Breakfast, Saturday 9/20 @ 9AM

Lancaster Baptist Church • 4020 E. Lancaster Blvd. • Lancaster, CA 93535
661.946.4663 • lancasterbaptist.org • Paul Chappell, Pastor

---

sample enrollment card

This enables our soulwinning director to partner soulwinners according to their adult Bible class as well as their level of skill. This means that new soulwinners will get partnered with experienced soulwinners for personal training, and everyone will be partnered with someone able to go at the same time of week who is from his adult Bible class—someone he already knows and with whom he has a connection. We also divide the doorknocking efforts in our community by adult

Bible classes, so for simple logistics, we want to keep members of the same class together.

Now, back to our four-word strategy…

TIMES—PROVIDE MULTIPLE SOULWINNING OPPORTUNITIES

Not everyone in your church will be free to go out soulwinning on Saturday mornings at 10:00. By scheduling multiple soulwinning times when you have soulwinning maps and visits ready, more people will be able to attend. I suggest every church begin with a minimum of two scheduled soulwinning times: Saturday mornings and a weekday evening.[2] From there, you can add more as you have opportunity. Our current soulwinning times are as follows:

- Wednesday morning soulwinning (held directly after my wife teaches a weekly ladies Bible study)
- Wednesday evening (This gathering is actually held in two locations—one at our church and one at a church member's home in West Palmdale, about fifteen miles from church. This is convenient for our members in Palmdale and allows them to maximize the daylight time in soulwinning rather than driving.)
- Saturday morning soulwinning and bus calling

The midweek evening and Saturday morning soulwinning have long been the staple soulwinning times for our church. Generally, we use Saturday morning to reach as many new houses through doorknocking as we can, and we use Wednesday evening to follow up on recent guests or doorknocking prospects.

Each of the soulwinning meetings is conducted by one of our pastoral staff. The meetings are exciting but brief. We sing a congregational song with an emphasis on salvation or soulwinning, and the leader gives a quick challenge from Scripture regarding soulwinning. This challenge usually holds a nugget of soulwinning instruction as well.

From there, soulwinners pair up and go out to knock on doors or make follow-up visits. Because of our method of having soulwinners partnered through the adult Bible classes, members who come to one of our soulwinning rallies generally already have a partner and are good to go. Sometimes, however, there will be people who do not have partners, and we'll either partner them together (if at least one of them is an experienced soulwinner), or we'll invite them to join another group.

Some churches re-partner people randomly each week. I prefer to encourage our members to have an established soulwinning partner for a particular season (from fall to spring and from spring to fall) and then get a new partner for the next season. This allows for consistent training of a new soulwinner as he has an established trainer/partner. It also encourages experienced soulwinners to regularly be looking for new people to train as they seek out new partners for the next season. And, finally, it encourages accountability for both partners.

Following the rally, we ask soulwinners to bring back their completed maps or visits and report how many doors they knocked, how many people were saved, how the visits went, etc. These reports not only encourage accountability, but they provide our church office with important statistics regarding the speed with which we're reaching the homes in our community as well as contact information for continued stewardship of prospects.

SUPPLIES—PREPARE SOULWINNING MAPS

We have taken a large map of our community—the Antelope Valley—and divided it into sections, assigning each section to a particular adult Bible class. Within these sections, we print out smaller maps and highlight individual streets. Those highlighted maps are placed in the soulwinning baskets for each adult Bible class. (In the early years of our church, we couldn't cover the entire valley, so we mapped the neighborhoods closest to the church. As we were able, we widened our circle of what we included in our maps.)

When a soulwinner comes to the soulwinning rally to go doorknocking, he is given a map with one or two streets (depending on the length of the street) highlighted. The highlighted street is his target for that time of soulwining.

Preparing and highlighting maps have worked very well for our church for several reasons. First, it eliminates time and decisions for the soulwinners preparing to go out. When soulwinners arrive at a church meeting, they are given a map from their soulwinning basket and they pick up a stack of tracts from the table in the back—no wasted time deciding where to go.

Second, and most obvious, the maps allow us to be strategic and thorough in reaching the homes in our community. Without the maps, some streets (especially near the church) would be knocked every few weeks—aggravating the residents—while other streets (further from the church) would be neglected entirely. Using the maps has helped us ensure that we are reaching our entire community.

Third, the maps have enabled us to assign areas of our community to specific adult Bible classes. This encourages a stewardship mentality as each class leader challenges his class to "own" their area. It also provides for convenient follow up in conjunction with future doorknocking.

As a final note on the maps, highlighting the printed maps is not a one-time event. You'll want to highlight fresh maps each time your church (or a particular class) completes their targeted area. We typically use a new color of highlighter for each successive round of maps so old maps don't get confused with new maps. Highlighting these maps has proved to be a welcome job for volunteers and a great way for people to be involved.

INSTRUCTION—PROVIDE THOROUGH TRAINING

Following the soulwinning kickoff, we hold elective training classes on Thursday evenings concurrent with our midweek church service. The classes run for eight consecutive weeks and are designed for people who want to learn *how* to be a soulwinner while at the same time have opportunity to *be* a soulwinner. In other words, we don't want a member who signs up for the class to wait until he completes the class to begin soulwinning. We encourage him to go out soulwinning with an experienced soulwinner on Saturday mornings or Wednesday evenings. Taking the elective class and having a personal on-the-job mentor during a soulwinning time provides tremendous experience and motivation for him to learn and grow.

Presently, we offer two classes for these electives: Evangelism 101 and Evangelism 401. The first class teaches students how to present the gospel, how to follow up on a prospect, and how to explain baptism and discipleship to a new convert. This class uses *To Seek and To Save*—a manual on soulwinning that I wrote for our church family—as a textbook.[3] Our soulwinning director teaches through the book, and each person in attendance receives a workbook that follows the lessons in the book. The Evangelism 401 class deals with more complex soulwinning issues, including how to witness to a Jehovah's Witness, a Mormon, etc.

In the early years of our church—before we had someone available to teach an elective class on evangelism—I taught through the *To Seek and To Save* material on Saturday mornings before we went out soulwinning. I would teach through a lesson in the book, and then we would partner up and knock on doors together.

In whatever way you provide soulwinning training, you want to be sure that soulwinners are given opportunity to actually go out soulwinning during the weeks in which they are attending the training. An effective soulwinning program will fuse together biblical teaching (the kickoff service), training (classes), and opportunity (soulwinning with a trainer/partner) all at the same time.

PROGRAM—TEAM SOULWINNING

When we started our soulwinning program, we called it TEAM—Training Every Available Member. In our kickoff service, I stress that it is everyone's responsibility to witness for Christ—that is not just a job for the pastor or the church staff. As I mentioned earlier, I believe my job is to equip every Christian in our church to share their faith, but it is everyone's responsibility to do it.

Our soulwinning program itself consists of both doorknocking and follow up. We refer to those who go doorknocking on a given week as "TEAM 1" and those who make follow-up calls as "TEAM 2."

TEAM 1

Those who are going out doorknocking need a partner and a map (as described above). When they return to the church, we ask that they turn in their maps, notating whether or not they completed the entire map. We also ask that they note how many doors they knocked on as well as how many people trusted Christ.

Later in the week, a church secretary or a volunteer will count up the total number of doors knocked and number of people saved and type this information into a database to help us track our efforts as a church family.

TEAM 2

Often, churches that are aggressive in door-to-door soulwinning tend to let the follow up of contacts slip through the cracks. But a truly effective church soulwinning program will include a plan for stewarding every contact God brings. In Chapter 9 we looked at the importance of *personally* stewarding contacts by maintaining an updated prospect list. Here, we see the importance of *corporately* stewarding contacts as a church family. In other words, we want a plan that multiple people share for following up on the guests God brings into the church or contacts given to the church. These contacts included in the soulwinning baskets may include any of the following:

- Guests in church services
- Contacts from soulwinners' personal prospect lists
- New move ins to the community[4]
- Other miscellaneous contacts shared by church members

The key word for TEAM 2 soulwinning is *diligence*. As I described in Chapter 9, we must be tenacious in our follow up of contacts. Every name represents a person—a person who needs Christ. Thus, our goal is not just to visit them once and check their name off our list. It is to follow up on them until the person is saved and added to the church.

At Lancaster Baptist, we have developed a thorough strategy for follow up. It is intense, but over the years, it has also been very fruitful.

On the next page is a chart that describes our process.

LifeStages Soulwinning Follow-Up Procedure

Visitor turns in visitor card at Worship Service

Visitor's information is recorded on stat sheet

Visitor information is entered in database for tracking

Visitor is assigned to a class leader for follow up

This assignment is based on LifeStages (age divisions on visitor card match class age divisions).

Follow-up visit is given to leader with map attached

Visit is made and results are reported to soulwinning secretary

Visit information is entered into database

Status reports are given to Pastor, showing results of visits

These reports are updated and given to Pastor twice a week.

Visitor remains on leader's prospect list until he becomes a member

Here is how this process plays out during a typical week:

1. Monday: Collect visitor cards from Sunday services and other contacts (new move ins, doorknocking referrals, etc.)

2. Monday: Create a master list for pastoral reviews.

3. Monday/Tuesday: Create individual cards with maps attached for home visits.

4. Tuesday: Distribute individual cards to the adult Bible class leaders.

5. Midweek soulwinning: Class leaders give cards to soulwinners at scheduled soulwinning meetings.

6. Midweek soulwinning: Visits are made, and results are reported to the soulwinning secretary.

7. Thursday/Friday: Visit information is entered into a database.

8. Friday: The master list is updated to see which visits need to be redistributed on Saturday. (Steps 4 through 7 are repeated for these visits, with the weekdays adjusted.)

9. Saturday and forward: Visitor remains on the class leader's prospect list until the visitor becomes a member.

As you can see, we follow the initial contact of a prospect (either from out soulwinning or a visitor to the church) through a series of checkpoints until that person has had an opportunity to hear the gospel, has been enrolled in an adult Bible class, and has joined the church. This level of tracking is a corporate responsibility that the local body must take very seriously. It requires that everyone involved be diligent in making visits, reporting results, and following up.

DREAM NO SMALL DREAMS

What is the goal of all of this detail, all of this planning, all of this organization?

Is it so our churches grow? No, a soulwinning church will grow, but we don't build a soulwinning program with the goal of growth. Frankly, that's not our responsibility. Acts 2:47 tells us, "And *the Lord* added to the church daily such as should be saved."

Our goal is simple, yet large. It is to reach people for Christ.

This is no small dream—no little undertaking.

But it is a *worthwhile* dream, for Jesus Himself came "to seek and to save that which was lost" (Luke 19:10).

Indeed, our goal—in our lives and in our churches—is Christlikeness. And what is more like Christ than reaching the lost?

As God gives us the privilege to witness for Him and to see people come to Christ, it is then our responsibility to help these new believers join in the process of developing Christlikeness. This is the privilege of discipleship—a vital part of reproducing soulwinners. And this leads us to our next chapter.

---

1   For a full-length book on biblical missions strategy, see *Sending Forth Laborers* (Striving Together Publications, 2007).

2   For many years, our weekday evening was on Tuesdays, and our church midweek service was on Wednesdays. This year, we moved our midweek service to Thursday evening and our midweek soulwinning to Wednesday evening.

3   *To Seek and To Save* is available in both English and Spanish through Striving Together Publications.

4   Names and addresses of new move-ins are available from a variety of sources. Our church currently uses Homeowners Marketing Services: www.homeownersmarketingservices.com.

THIRTEEN

THE PRIORITY
OF DISCIPLESHIP

Because Edwards Air Force Base is just twenty-five miles from our church, it is not uncommon for families stationed at the base to visit Lancaster Baptist. In late 1986, just months after I moved to Lancaster, Al Price was one of those visitors.

Al was a Staff Sergeant (E-5) in the Air Force when he and his wife, Trish, and their two children moved to California for Al's assignment at Edwards. The Tuesday evening after the Price family visited, I drove out to their home on the base to visit with them. Al had grown up in church, and he told me he was saved. Trish shared that she had been saved as a child. They were excited to find a new church home.

What Al had not counted on, however, was the directness of the gospel preaching at our church. Every Sunday, as he and Trish drove back to the base, they would fight—Al insisting that Trish had to be telling me everything about him and Trish denying the claims. The truth was that Al had never been saved, and the preaching was convicting his heart.

Al travelled heavily for the military on classified assignments. He would leave every Sunday evening and return Friday evening. This meant he would only attend Sunday morning church—a secret relief to him.

But one Sunday morning after service, I gave Al a stack of cassette tapes. (Yes, this was before the days of CDs.) Sincerely believing I was doing Al a favor, I mentioned I didn't want him to have to be without preaching while he was away so much and that I hoped the tapes would be a blessing to him.

As usual, Al and Trish fought on the drive home—first about the sermon and now about why I gave him the tapes. Once home, Al began packing his bags for the week's assignment. As he packed, a ritual began that would last for a solid year. Trish brought the stack of tapes I had given Al and set them in his suitcase. When Trish left the room, Al took them out. When Al wasn't looking, Trish put them in. He took them back out. She put them in. No matter how many times Trish put the tapes in or Al took them out, when Al arrived at his destination Sunday evening and opened his suitcase, the tapes were always there—every Sunday for a year.

Eventually, Al dropped out of church entirely. I prayed for him, and I did what I could to encourage him, but he just wasn't interested. He recently reminded me that I called him once on a Sunday morning five minutes before the service started, just to say, "Al, I just wanted you to know I miss you being here." The call meant a lot to him.

Not long after, Al woke up one Saturday night to the sound of someone crying beside his bed. It was Trish. Pretending to remain asleep, Al heard her praying, "Lord, please get ahold of my husband's heart. I don't think he's saved. Please save him."

The following afternoon, Al and Trish resumed their ritual of putting the preaching tapes in the suitcase and removing them again. They had done this for a year, and Trish always won…but Al still had not listened to a single tape.

That evening, at the hotel room near Al's classified assignment, Al was having trouble sleeping. It was in May—around high school graduation time. In the room next door, a group of teens were partying it up loudly. Al asked them to quiet down, but it didn't do any good. As the night wore on, their party increased in volume. Unable to take it any longer, Al hurled his heavy combat boot against the door connecting the two rooms and hollered at them to shut up so he could sleep. It didn't phase them for a second.

In complete frustration, it occurred to Al that since he couldn't sleep anyway, he may as well get up and listen to one of the preaching tapes. It turned out to be the testimony of Evangelist Carl Hatch whose life story was so similar to Al's that it caught his attention. When the tape was over, Al was filled with conviction—and with a desire to be saved. He called me from his motel room, and I had the joy of leading him to Christ on the phone.

The following Sunday, Al asked me to baptize him. What I didn't know was that he hadn't yet told Trish that he had been saved! Her surprise and delight was a church memory none of us will ever forget—especially Trish. She hasn't let Al live it down.

After salvation, Al's life transformed. He grew spiritually from the inside out—and he just couldn't get enough preaching. He continued to travel for the military, and he frequently asked me for preaching tapes to bring with him. We did not yet have a formal discipleship program at our church, but I did everything I could to encourage Al's growth. He began going soulwinning with me, and I took the opportunities to mentor him spiritually.

It was a sad day three years later when the military moved the Price family to Missouri. They quickly found a good Bible-preaching church and continued growing in their Christian walk. While in Missouri, Al sensed the call of God on his life to preach.

Five years later, Al and Trish returned to Lancaster—this time to enroll in West Coast Baptist College. They graduated and launched out into a life of ministry.

A few years ago, I received a call from Al. I remember how my heart leapt when he told me God was burdening his heart to plant a church. I couldn't help but think back to the day when I first sat in Al's living room with an open Bible and then the night over a year later when he called to tell me that he wanted to be saved. I couldn't help but think back to the sweet times of fellowship and discipleship mentoring Al and I had shared. And I couldn't help but wonder what his life would look like today without the soulwinning and growth opportunities of our church.

Al's testimony speaks to so many sides of the soulwinning equation: It speaks of the need for true gospel preaching. (This is what first began to convict Al of his need for salvation.) It speaks of the power of a wife's faithful, compassionate prayers. It speaks of the importance of being kindly tenacious in follow up, even when there is little to no response. It speaks of the power of the gospel to change a life. And it speaks of the importance of encouraging continued growth in a young Christian's life.

Today, Al Price pastors Naples Bible Baptist Church, which God used him to plant, in Naples, Florida. But it may not have ended that way.

From the day when I first drove out to visit Al on the base until the day he called me from his hotel room, my primary objective was to see him trust Christ as his Saviour. But that wasn't my *final* objective. Had I hung up the phone after he was saved without ever pointing him to be baptized as a first step of growth, he very well may never have told Trish he was saved! And after he was baptized, had our church family neglected to encourage him in his continued growth, I wonder where he would be today? Perhaps the same place as too many young Christians who are won to Christ through aggressive soulwinning but then neglected by those who led them to Christ.

Discipleship is vital to our obedience to the Great Commission. Actually, it is *part* of the Great Commission: "Teaching them to observe all things whatsoever I have commanded you..." (Matthew 28:20).

Second Timothy 2:2—a verse that is the theme verse for our discipleship ministry—further instructs, "And the things that thou hast heard of me among many witnesses, the same commit thou to faithful men, who shall be able to teach others also."

We simply cannot lead people to Christ and then neglect these new babes in Christ. We must have a strategic plan for discipleship.

THE RESPONSIBILITY OF NEW LIFE

In the parable Christ told of the lost sheep, He described the incredible lengths to which a shepherd will go to seek out a missing sheep: "What man of you, having an hundred sheep, if he lose one of them, doth not leave the ninety and nine in the wilderness, and go after that which is lost, until he find it?" (Luke 15:4). From Christ's words, we are reminded of the priority of seeking the lost and leading them to Christ through soulwinning.

But Jesus didn't end the story there. He pointed out that a shepherd having found a lost sheep is willing to bear the burden of this needy animal: "And when he hath found it, he layeth it on his shoulders, rejoicing." *This* is discipleship. Even as it is the responsibility of a shepherd to care for a found lamb, it is the responsibility of a soulwinner to care for a new Christian.

Consider another analogy, one with which you may be more familiar. Think of a father holding a newborn son or daughter and envisioning the future for his little one. In that moment, the father makes a personal pledge to fully invest himself into the child's future.

Similarly, each person who trusts Christ as Saviour is immediately made a new creature in Christ. Second Corinthians 5:17 says it plainly: "Therefore if any man be in Christ, he is a new creature: old things are passed away; behold, all things are become new."

This new Christian, however, doesn't possess immediate spiritual maturity. Hebrews 5:13 says, "For every one that useth milk is unskilful in the word of righteousness: for he is a babe." Spiritual maturity—like personal maturity—isn't an automatic process. Discipleship is the process of guiding a young Christian into spiritual maturity.

Intentional discipleship is the model of ministry we see in the New Testament. Think about it: Jesus had twelve disciples. And as you read through the book of Acts, you don't get the sense that young Christians were left to themselves after salvation. Rather, you see them assembling daily in close fellowship as young Christians were mentored and trained.

To what extent do you suppose Paul would have grown had not Barnabas discipled him? What if Paul had not discipled Timothy and Titus? Only God knows. In the end, every Christian's spiritual growth takes place because of the work of the Holy Spirit within, and it is all to the glory of God. But in God's plan, this growth takes place through the personal transfer of discipleship.

Understand, however, that when I speak of discipling new Christians, I'm not speaking *only* of an organized, formal discipleship (although I believe that is important). I'm speaking of the full process of bringing a young believer on in his Christian life—giving him the tools and encouragement he needs to grow. This is larger than a once-per-week formal discipleship meeting. It is a multifaceted, full-church endeavor of reproducing committed followers of Jesus Christ.

What does it require? I believe it requires three biblical components—an atmosphere of growth, a spirit of hospitality, and an equipped church.

AN ATMOSPHERE OF GROWTH

Like a greenhouse providing light and warmth to nurture growth, a local church should cultivate an atmosphere that is conducive to spiritual growth—an atmosphere where growth and lasting life changes are the most natural thing in the world.

What does this look like? What comprises an atmosphere of growth? Patience. Biblical growth takes place from the inside out. This means that young Christians need patience as the Holy Spirit works from within.

Sure, we could rush this process by placing an emphasis on the exterior and urging young Christians to immediately conform. But in so doing, we'd be stunting the long-term growth that comes only through a patient process.

Growth takes time, and so we must give new Christians time to "grow in grace, and in the knowledge of our Lord and Saviour Jesus Christ" (2 Peter 3:18).

What does this patience look like in real life? Love. It is the willingness to love fledgling believers right where they are and just as they are—while at the same time mentoring them in the process of being transformed to the image of Christ.

An atmosphere of patient love is an atmosphere of acceptance. In our zeal to see outward manifestations of growth, sometimes we fail to accept people, and we unconsciously communicate rejection—or conditional acceptance—to them.

Obviously, I am not speaking of condoning sin or supporting someone in a sinful lifestyle. Indeed, part of discipleship involves confronting sin and giving scriptural teaching on holiness and biblical separation. Consider for a moment, however, those who have had the greatest impact on your Christian growth. Were they constantly "on your case"? Or did you sense from them a patient love and committed acceptance?

Acceptance is the optimum environment for growth. It nurtures the heart as the Holy Spirit works from within.

A SPIRIT OF HOSPITALITY

Discipleship doesn't just happen in the pew on Sunday morning. Nor does it take place only in weekly meetings scheduled for "discipleship." Discipleship takes place when a mature Christian transfers biblical truth to the heart and mind of a young Christian. Discipleship happens whenever 2 Timothy 2:2 is being followed: "And the things that thou hast heard of me among many witnesses, the same commit thou to faithful men, who shall be able to teach others also."

One of the most significant opportunities for discipleship is personal hospitality. Many new Christians have never been in a home where the husband and wife have a loving marriage within the context of the biblical roles of marriage. They haven't seen a home free of trashy pop culture or suggestive art or entertainment. They don't know what Christian fellowship looks like outside the confines of shaking hands in church.

Christian hospitality provides a model of Christian living. (Don't misunderstand that word *model* to mean you must be near-perfect to invite people over. Think of it more like a music teacher playing a piece for a student. The teacher knows that he is no concert musician. He sees his flaws, and he practices to continue to develop his own skill. But he also realizes that he is further along than the student and that by playing the piece for the student, he provides a helpful model for the student.)

Hospitality opens hearts. When you invite someone to your home, you invite them into your life. And that invitation opens a heart.

No wonder the New Testament emphasizes hospitality as a necessary qualification for spiritual leaders and as an instruction to all Christians:

> *Use hospitality one to another without grudging.* —1 PETER 4:9

> *Distributing to the necessity of saints; given to hospitality.*—ROMANS 12:13

> *A bishop then must be blameless, the husband of one wife, vigilant, sober, of good behaviour, given to hospitality, apt to teach;*— 1 TIMOTHY 3:2

Opening your home never happens by accident. (Ask my wife.) It requires time, planning, and genuine care.

At Lancaster Baptist Church, we encourage every deacon, adult Bible class leader, and discipler to develop a spirit of hospitality toward those they lead and mentor. In recent years, we've added a layer of intentionality by scheduling two church-wide home fellowship nights each year. These take place after the Sunday evening service in the homes of our adult Bible class leaders. Large classes divide and fellowship in multiple homes within the class as we want each group to remain small enough for real fellowship to take place.

But twice a year isn't enough. It's simply a start—and a good way to be sure everyone in the church is included in hospitality *at least* that often. My wife and I often invite various groups from our church family—especially newer Christians—over to our home after the Sunday evening service. Other times we'll take a newer family out to lunch. As a personal checkpoint, we schedule hospitality at a minimum of two Sundays out of four.

In addition to the hospitality expressed by opening your home, develop the hospitality of inclusion—including new Christians in everything you do. For instance, ask a newer Christian to be your soulwinning partner. Invite a new believer to go with you to make Sunday school class visits. Ask him to join you in serving in church ministry on Sundays.

Consider the discipleship model between Paul and Timothy. Near the end of his life, Paul was able to say to Timothy, "But thou hast fully known my doctrine, manner of life, purpose, faith, longsuffering, charity, patience" (2 Timothy 3:10). How did Timothy "fully know" everything about Paul—from his teachings to his lifestyle to his personal responses? Because as Paul trained Timothy, he opened his life to him. This openness— this hospitality of heart—facilitates biblical discipleship.

A CHURCH EQUIPPED TO DISCIPLE

As vital as an atmosphere of acceptance and a spirit of hospitality are to discipleship, real discipleship does not take place simply by osmosis. There must be specific processes that are pursued with passion by the church family. Churches that are serious about obeying the Great Commission not only believe in 2 Timothy 2:2, they have a strategy for developing the relationships and authentic church life that makes this verse a reality.

At our church, that process is threefold: adult Bible classes, a new members' class, and formal discipleship training.

ADULT BIBLE CLASSES

Adult Bible classes (which we sometimes refer to as Sunday school classes or adult Bible fellowships) should be greenhouses of dynamic spiritual growth. They provide opportunity for connection and close mentoring. They are the most natural setting through which to forge the kind of spiritually strengthening and challenging relationships admonished in Hebrews 10:24–25: "And let us consider one another to provoke unto love and to good works: Not forsaking the assembling of ourselves together, as the manner of some is; but exhorting one another: and so much the more, as ye see the day approaching."

At Lancaster Baptist, the adult Bible classes are the hub of our church. They facilitate the organization needed to accomplish the purpose of the church—reaching people with the gospel and discipling them in Christian growth. When our church was young, I was the only adult Bible class teacher. As the church grew and as leaders were being mentored from within the church, we found it helpful to divide into additional classes. We have structured these classes according to life stages, adding classes over the years for single adults, young married couples, median couples, seniors, etc.

We encourage every guest in our services to attend an adult Bible class. And the first week they attend a class, we encourage them to enroll. Class enrollment does not make them a member of the church, so it is not even necessary that they are saved and baptized to be enrolled. Inviting them to enroll lets them know that a smaller group of people within our church wants to include them and feels that they belong. It encourages them to feel somewhat committed to the class as well.

Class leaders are responsible to diligently follow up on guests of their classes in the process described in our previous chapter—finding out if they're saved, sharing the gospel with them, leading them to Christ, explaining baptism, etc. After a person is saved and baptized, the class leader will encourage him to begin formal discipleship with another member (or couple if a husband and wife are beginning discipleship together) of the class.

Adult Bible classes provide a structure—not only for the regular soulwinning mentioned in our previous chapter—but also for tenacious follow up and then careful discipleship. They provide an entry point into a community of people who will cultivate the atmosphere of growth and spirit of hospitality mentioned earlier.

NEW MEMBERS' CLASS

Every few months I have the privilege of teaching a three-week class at our church for new or prospective members. I relish this time with newcomers to our church, and I've found they thoroughly enjoy it as well. This class is designed to help orientate a new Christian (or someone new to our church) in biblical doctrine, our ministry philosophy, and discipleship. It also allows those in the class and me to become better acquainted with one another.

In the earliest days of our church, our new members' orientation consisted of an afternoon reception at our home. Terrie and I would set up chairs in the living room and provide food for fellowship. We both would share our testimonies, and I would explain to our new members the structure and vision of our church. I'd share our Baptist distinctives with them, express my heart to be available for their spiritual needs, and give them an opportunity to ask questions.

Over the years, this new member orientation has evolved.[1] Currently we offer it as a three-week class during our normal Sunday school hour (those attending the class leave their regular adult Bible class for three weeks to do so), and we call it "Starting Point."

- On week 1, I teach about the story of Lancaster Baptist Church—our history as well as the main biblical distinctives of our church.
- On week 2, I teach about life in the family of Lancaster Baptist. This includes our threefold purpose statement (loving God, growing together, serving others) with practical applications for being part of these areas.
- On week 3, I teach about the biblical structure of a church as well as specifics of what this looks like in our church. I explain the offices of the pastor and deacon, give them information regarding who they can contact for help, and encourage them to fully engage in one of the adult Bible classes.

In our church, we encourage new members as well as potential members to attend "Starting Point." Often, the potential members make the decision to join the church at some point during this class.

On the Sunday evening following the final class, I introduce the new members to our church family at the close of the evening service. After the service, members are encouraged to greet the new members. This allows our existing members to reach out to the newcomers with a warm welcome. It also allows newcomers to begin forming new relationships.

Whatever your strategy for orientating new members to your church family, it is absolutely imperative that you do have some strategy.

DISCIPLESHIP TRAINING

We started our formal discipleship training over fifteen years ago, and I can't stress strongly enough how it has helped develop spiritual maturity in our new Christians. I can see a marked difference in the attrition rate of new Christians in our church from before we began formal discipleship and after we began discipleship. In the early days of our church, I could easily have the church over to my home regularly and spend time with each of the men in our church on a fairly regular basis providing mentoring and discipleship. As our church grew, however, it became more difficult to intentionally lead each new Christian to the next step of spiritual growth.

In a formal discipleship program, a new Christian has a personal one-on-one mentor teaching him the basics of the Christian life. Our discipleship program[2] includes lessons on the Bible, who God is, salvation and assurance of salvation, cultivating a daily devotional life, spiritual victory and holy living, the local church, Christian relationships, financial stewardship, and much more. For a young Christian to have a seasoned Christian teach basic lessons in a structured, committed format is invaluable to his Christian growth.

A thorough discipleship curriculum will not be completed in four or five sessions. It is long enough to allow the discipler and the disciple to develop a relationship of mentoring, encouragement, trust, and friendship. A three-lesson pamphlet may give scriptural basis for the tenants of the faith, but it does not allow for developing a relationship that grounds a new believer in truth.

An effective curriculum will also be steeped in Scripture. The goal of discipleship is to teach a young Christian what we believe *from the Bible.* It's not a bulleted list of principles; it's a biblical foundation for the Christian life and for developing a daily walk with the Lord.

In the process of discipleship, disciplers invite their disciples to participate in soulwinning—usually offering to take the disciple with them. Toward the end of the program, disciplers encourage their disciples to serve in some form of church ministry—ushering, choir, children's classes,[3] etc. This helps new Christians assimilate into the church family and to begin practical obedience to the Great Commission themselves.

On a practical note of logistics, we conduct our discipleship program during our regular midweek service. The benefits to this schedule include having childcare available and the disciplers from our church family not being asked to add another evening of ministry to their schedules. Additionally, the disciple develops a habit of attending the midweek service and usually makes a smooth transition from discipleship into the auditorium Bible study. (We actually present a certificate of completion to a disciple in the auditorium the week following his final lesson of discipleship.)

ADDITION VS. MULTIPLICATION

Some Christians, even some churches, who are diligent and purposeful in soulwinning, are hesitant to engage in structured discipleship. They fear that discipleship will distract them from reaching new people for Christ. To make their case, they often point to the regular preaching of God's Word in church as being sufficient for a young Christian to become grounded in the faith.

I appreciate any concern that is motivated by a desire to guard soulwinning and reaching lost people for Christ. If we neglect soulwinning, only turning inward in a continual "discipleship" of those who are already part of our churches, we have neglected obedience to Christ's command.

However, I believe that a balanced, biblically rooted discipleship program will not undermine soulwinning efforts—it will multiply them. Not only can fervent soulwinning and focused discipleship coexist—they should complement each other. Indeed, this is what we see in the book of Acts. The Christians were diligent in their evangelism efforts, and God blessed, adding new Christians (Acts 2:42, 5:42). But it didn't stop there. As the churches took care to teach the new believers, "the number of the disciples was multiplied" (Acts 6:1, also see Acts 6:7).

Biblical discipleship elevates soulwinning from the level of *addition* to *multiplication*. The fruit of discipleship is more Christians with a fruitful Christian walk engaged in sharing their faith. And this multiplication effect means that more lost sheep are found.

---

1   For a more in-depth treatment of a new members class, check the free Spiritual Leadership Podcast, "How to Host a New Members Orientation": http://www.paulchappell.com/2012/04/25/spiritual-leadership-podcast-how-to-host-a-new-members-orientation/

2   Visit strivingtogether.com for discipleship resources.

3   For the protection of children, we do have careful policies in place for our children's ministries, including a full background check for anyone desiring to serve in nursery or children's classes.

FOURTEEN

SOULWINNING AND SPECIAL DAYS IN THE LOCAL CHURCH

It was October 4, 1986—less than three months after our family had moved to Lancaster to pastor a church of fewer than twenty people. We had been diligent in our soulwinning, and God was blessing our efforts. In less than three months, the church had grown to average about fifty in Sunday morning attendance.

But I believed God wanted to do more through our church, and I asked our church family to plan an upcoming special Sunday for our community, an "Open House." The date we planned was October 5.

The last week of September and first few days of October found us busy. We extended our usually planned Tuesday evening/Saturday morning soulwinning times to every night of the week (except Wednesday) and most of the day on Saturday. Over the course of a couple of weeks, we invited thousands of people to come.

On Saturday evening, October 4, we had a prayer meeting for the big day. I remember kneeling on the cement floor with Bill Weible (Bill and his wife, Fran, were two of the members of the church who were there when I came) and praying for God to bless the services on Sunday. In fact, I prayed an audacious prayer—I asked God to bring one hundred people the following day.

As usual on Sunday mornings, I arrived early to church. I was still asking the Lord for an attendance of one hundred, but I wasn't so sure. Shortly before the service started, however, guests began pouring in. The building had more people in it than we had ever seen, and we were thrilled! I preached a gospel message, and several people trusted Christ as Saviour. I knew that, regardless of the attendance count, the Lord had blessed this Sunday, and we were going to do it every year.

After the service, I asked the usher who counted attendance how many had come. One hundred and one. I was ecstatic! Not only had God answered our prayer for one hundred, but He had given one more.

But that's not the end of the story. Fast forward three weeks to October 26, 1986, and the attendance log shows an even greater surprise—157. Remember, October 26 wasn't an "Open House" Sunday. It was just an "ordinary" Sunday. Why did so many guests come?

I believe the answer lies in the philosophy with which we approached the special Sunday. For us, Open House wasn't simply a day to reach as many people as we could, rejoice in the number of people saved, and then move on to find more people. We viewed it as an opportunity to invite people to a specific

Sunday, preach the gospel, and follow up on the guests who came as well as those who said they might come but didn't. The high attendance on October 26 (150 percent of the high attendance on October 5) was the fruit of aggressive soulwinning *and* diligent follow up. It was also a pointed indicator of the value of special Sundays in reaching people with the gospel.

Days with special emphasis for the local church can bear long-lasting fruit. There are *hundreds* of people in our church today who have been reached over the past twenty-eight years on our Open House Sunday, at a Christmas musical, Friend Day, or another special event.

I believe in creating and hosting special days in the church. I believe they provide a tremendous strategy for reaching the community, including new soulwinners in a great endeavor, and encouraging a church family to reach friends and family for Christ. In this chapter, I'd like to give you an overview of how to use special days as a tool for outreach, how to prepare for them, and how to follow up on guests.

IDEAS

We have used different special days over the years, but for the most part, we've settled on a core set:

Friend Day—Members invite friends…or anyone they can convince to be their friends! This can include neighbors, business acquaintances, etc.

First Responder Sunday—We make a special effort to reach the law enforcement officers and first responders in our community. This year, we are specifically inviting nurses as well. We show our appreciation to them in the service and invite each department to recognize an outstanding member of their department.

Country Harvest Days—This is the entire month of October. The second or third Sunday of the month is Open House Sunday (see next), but we have something special going on each Sunday of the month.

Open House/Love Works—Historically, Open House Sunday has been the largest Sunday of the year as far as the number of homes we reach with invitations and the number of guests who come. We have a meal after the service for guests and those who brought them. Last year, we shifted the name and the focus of this Sunday and called it Love Works Sunday. (We'll look at this in more detail in Chapter 15.)

Neighborhood Impact Sunday—As our church has grown, we reached a point when it became impractical because of limited space to include our bus ministry in the Open House Sunday emphasis. (We still run the buses on Open House, but our emphasis for the day is for drive-in guests.) Our bus emphasis Sunday is in the spring, and we call it Neighborhood Impact Sunday as we canvass neighborhoods inviting new riders and their parents.

Easter/Christmas musicals—Twice a year—a Saturday evening and Sunday morning in December and the evening before Easter and Easter Sunday—we have a musical or program with a gospel message to which we invite our community. After the program, I preach the gospel, usually in about a twenty-minute sermon. We have seen great fruit from these programs.

I'd like to note here that when I say we "invite the community," I don't mean we simply post an invitation to our church Facebook page. We literally *go* invite the community—door to door and through personal relationships.

RELATIONAL OPPORTUNITIES

Relationships are important to the spreading of the gospel. In fact, the relationships God has given us with unsaved people are a responsibility, and it is vital that we cultivate them toward sharing the truth of the gospel.

Jesus Himself associated with and graciously touched those who needed salvation. Andrew invited his brother, Peter, to Christ (John 1:41). The woman at the well brought an entire village to come hear Christ (John 4:39). When Christ loosed the demoniac of Gadara, He instructed him, "Go home to thy friends, and tell them how great things the Lord hath done for thee, and hath had compassion on thee" (Mark 5:19).

One of the blessings of special days in the church is that they provide good opportunities for these relational-orientated invitations. For instance, I don't invite my neighbors to church every time I see them. (That would be a great way to destroy a relationship!) But I can easily invite them to a special service such as a Christmas musical or a Friend Day.

As we plan for special days at our church, we encourage our church family to use the opportunity to invite family members, coworkers, neighbors, friends, and other acquaintances. These days have proved to be incredibly fruitful in leading people to Christ with whom we've shared the gospel but aren't able to keep pushing for a response. These are also tremendous follow-up opportunities for people who are on a soulwinner's prospect list (described in Chapter 9) but have not yet come to church.

Additionally, events such as First Responder Sunday or Love Works Sunday provide specific opportunities to seek out and establish relationships for the cause of sharing the gospel.

GOSPEL SATURATION

Contrasted with the relational invitations of Andrew to Peter and the woman at the well to her friends and acquaintances, notice the saturation approach Jesus took when He sent out the seventy disciples: "After these things the Lord appointed other seventy also, and sent them two and two before his face into every city and place, whither he himself would come" (Luke 10:1).

This principle of saturation evangelism is vital for a church that wants to truly make an impact on its area for Christ.

While some special days are primarily relationally orientated in nature, most special days have the added opportunity of saturating the community with the gospel. In fact, this is one of our primary goals in Open House/Love Works Sunday and the Christmas/Easter musicals.

In the early years of our church, we would attempt to saturate entire neighborhoods—beginning with those neighborhoods closest to our church and reaching out as far as we could. In recent years, as our church has grown, we have saturated the entire population of our city and the three or four cities around us.

I believe these two aspects—relationships and blanket saturation—are seen in the life of Paul. Throughout the New

Testament we see people Paul befriended and personally led to Christ. We also see Paul's diligence in saturating entire regions with the gospel. In Romans 15:19, he wrote, "…from Jerusalem, and round about unto Illyricum, *I have fully preached the gospel of Christ.*"

A form of the word *fully* in Romans 15 is also found in John 12:3: "Then took Mary a pound of ointment of spikenard, very costly, and anointed the feet of Jesus, and wiped his feet with her hair: and the house was *filled* with the odour of the ointment." Have you ever spilled a bottle of cologne? Its fragrance saturates every odor-absorbing item nearby. This is the level of saturation with which Paul saturated areas with the gospel.

To understand the accuracy of what Paul said when he declared he had "fully preached the gospel," notice Romans 15:23, "But now having no more place in these parts…." From Jerusalem to Illyricum, there was no region untouched by the gospel. That's saturation evangelism!

This concept of saturation evangelism is why I began knocking on 500 doors per week for my first sixteen months in Lancaster. It is why our church family has collectively knocked on over 400,000 doors annually for nearly twenty years. Behind every door lives a person (or an entire family), and we believe it is vital to saturate the homes in our community with the gospel. I know this approach is considered out of touch with the times, but it is biblically based and historically proven. Just because the cults have adapted a biblical method doesn't mean we should abandon it.

Obviously, we can't dictate the response a person will have to the gospel. For this reason, saturation evangelism is not so much a church-building strategy as it is an obedience strategy. Like the seventy evangelists Jesus sent out, we are responsible only to share the truth. When people reject our message, we are guiltless for their response, but we know we have obeyed our orders.

And yet, as we are obedient, God *does* bless. As I mentioned earlier, there are hundreds of people in our church today who were reached through one of the special days—either because they were invited by a friend or by a soulwinner at their doorstep.

PRACTICAL HOW TOs

In the remainder of this chapter, I'd like to share with you some practical notes regarding preparing for, carrying out, and following up after special days.[1]

HOW TO PREPARE FOR A SPECIAL DAY

Once a church has a special day planned on the calendar, what can you—as a soulwinner—do to use that event fully to reach people for Christ? Below are ten suggestions:

Pray daily for souls. Every day, ask the Lord to give you opportunities to witness and to go before you to prepare and convict hearts.

Pray for God's power. The Holy Spirit is the real Soulwinner. Ask Him to fill you and to empower your efforts to reach people with the gospel.

Obey every impulse of the Holy Spirit. As important as it is to schedule time for soulwinning, the Holy Spirit doesn't work in hearts only on Saturday mornings and only on the specific street you are canvassing! Be sensitive and spontaneous when He prompts you to speak to someone, and be ready with gospel tracts and printed invitations to the upcoming special event.

Set goals. Is this an event to which you should invite personal acquaintances? Write down names of those you want to invite, and begin checking them off as you make phone calls, send emails, or stop by to visit. Is this an event for gospel saturation? While we have never set an attendance goal at Lancaster Baptist, I will encourage you to set goals for how many doors you want to knock on in the weeks leading up to the event, and share your goals with a friend for accountability.

Give the gospel. Although you are inviting people to a special event at church, seize the opportunity (especially when out doorknocking) to speak to them about salvation as well. I treat this canvassing in the same way as any other doorknocking—I'm not just inviting people to church, but I'm looking for a chance to share the gospel with them. If the timing isn't right, I don't push it, but I do look for opportunities.

Train your partner. If you are an experienced soulwinner, the evangelistic emphasis in preparing for a special event is a wonderful time to train your soulwinning partner. Because I schedule extra time for soulwinning before special events, I find it a good time to invite multiple people to come with me in a given week, providing additional opportunities for soulwinning training.

Cultivate your prospect list. When you're at someone's doorstep and they indicate they may come to church for the special event, graciously press for a commitment. Give them your phone number and ask for theirs so you can call the day before to remind them. Jot down their address and send them a card a few days later. Work to cultivate your prospect list with as great care as a salesman would use to cultivate his prospective sales list—only for a far greater purpose. (As an additional note, special events are also a great time to review your prospect list and follow up on old contacts.)

Ask your partner for the names of his friends. Prompt each other to think of friends or acquaintances either of you should be inviting. If you are training a young Christian, he may want you to go with him to give out the invitations.

Make Saturday night calls. Late afternoon or early evening before the special day, call through your prospect list to remind folks that you're looking forward to seeing them on Sunday. This takes only a few minutes, but it goes a long way toward bringing a prospect to church. (You might send them a reminder email on Friday or Saturday as well.)

Expect great blessings from God. William Carey famously said, "Expect great things from God; attempt great things for God." There is nothing greater than bringing souls to Christ, and you've spent weeks attempting the great. Now it is time to pray and expect God to work!

ON A SPECIAL DAY

Your work isn't over on Saturday evening. Sunday morning yields more opportunities to lead people to Christ. What can you do?

Meet your guests at church. As mentioned earlier, when you talk with prospective guests on Saturday, prearrange a place to meet on Sunday morning. Be waiting for them when they arrive at church. Save a seat early, and bring them right in. It's simple for you to do, but just having a caring person greet them and host them will go a long way toward taking away the edge of discomfort they will experience in visiting a new place—let alone a church.

Greet all guests at church. Some people will come simply because they found a flyer on their door and won't have a personal host. Be friendly to everyone, and do your best to introduce guests (your guests and other guests) to others.

Be prepared to counsel at the altar. Most likely, the sermon on a special day will be a gospel message for the unsaved. Be ready and available at the end of the message, when the pastor invites listeners to respond to the gospel, to help counsel your guests. If you are accustomed to using a marked Bible or New Testament in presenting the gospel, have that with you.

Look for opportunities to witness. Just because someone doesn't respond to the gospel at the end of the sermon doesn't mean they can't be saved! As the Lord allows and as you sense an openness in your guests or in others you meet, ask them about their salvation. At our annual Open House, we have a complimentary meal following the morning service for our guests and those who brought them. Every year, people are saved at the meal.

Begin lining up your follow-up visits. Each guest is a trust from God. Regardless of whether or not they trusted Christ, you need to continue to follow up on them. If they were saved on Sunday, you want to explain baptism to them. If they were not, you want a chance to sit down with them in their home to ask about their experience at church. Did they enjoy it? Did they understand the message? Do they have any questions? Have they made the decision to trust Christ as their Saviour? Undoubtedly, there will also be follow-up visits you will want to make to people who said they would come but then didn't. Don't drop these contacts just because the special day is past. Now is the time to steward these contacts for continued follow up and discipleship.

Give thanks to God! At the end of a special Sunday, when I have a chance to sit down and reflect on the day, I'm always humbled that God would use us and entrust us with spiritual fruit. Be sure to thank Him and give all the glory to Him for the great things He has done!

HOW TO FOLLOW UP AFTER A SPECIAL DAY

After a weekend of abundant fruitfulness, I not only feel grateful, I also feel very responsible. I want to follow up on guests and nurture young Christians to grow in Christ. I believe that "big days" of ministry must be just the starting point for continued discipleship and training. Aggressive soulwinning must be followed with aggressive discipleship. Second Timothy 2:2 makes it clear that our job is to "teach others also" in the things we have learned.

Below are admonitions for follow up after a special day:

Make follow-up calls. Often by Sunday evening, you've planned who from your personal prospect list you want to follow up on in the coming week. As visitor cards are collected, there may be more follow-up visits given out early in the week. Be sure to make those visits. I assume that if someone comes to a service, God is already working in his heart and that he has at least some level of a spiritual hunger for Him. When I make a follow-up call, I try to be friendly and even folksy, but I do bring the conversation to a spiritual focus—that's why I'm making the visit in the first place.

Biblically explain baptism. If your visit is to someone who has just been saved, take a few minutes to ask him what he understands about baptism and to explain its biblical significance from God's Word. Let him know that it is the first step of obedience to Christ after salvation. Take time to listen and to be sure he understands that while baptism is not part of salvation, it is also not an option, but rather a command for an obedient child of God.[2]

Extend hospitality. Encourage a guest to return by inviting him to your home (or offering to purchase his meal at a restaurant) after service the following Sunday. This is also a great time to invite others over, possibly another family who has something in common with your guest, so your guest gets acquainted with others in the church.

Include guests in an adult Bible class. Some guests, especially on their first Sunday, will come to the worship service but not a Sunday school class. Inviting them to come to a class is a great lead-in when you make a follow-up visit. It is also an important aspect to facilitate their forming relationships within the church. If you lead an adult Bible class, plan a class activity to take place two to three weeks after a special Sunday at church. This is a great way to include those newer to the church (as well as to reach out to brand-new guests).

Be diligent and kindly persistent. Whether it be a new convert or an unsaved person on your prospect list, patience is the key. Perhaps they will not come to church the first time they commit to come, or perhaps they won't trust Christ the first time they hear the gospel, but they may respond the third time...or the eighth! Be prayerful and patient.

CHURCH-WIDE BENEFITS OF SPECIAL DAYS

Special days always require some sacrifices to fulfill the mission. There are sacrifices of time and energy in knocking on doors, sending notes, making follow-up calls, and praying for a harvest. Yet, the sacrifices we make pale in comparison to the spiritual fruit they produce.

From a pastoral perspective, there are at least seven ways in which I have observed our church family engage to reach the lost on these days—and each one comes with accompanying blessings.

Feeling the burden—For several weeks prior to these special days, I preach about the burden of our Lord Jesus Christ for souls. It is a joy to see our church family recognizing that Jesus came to Earth to seek and to save the lost (Luke 19:10). It is a blessing to see them be moved to action with compassion, even as Jesus was moved with compassion (Matthew 9:36).

Sharing the vision—It is one thing to feel a burden; it is another thing to share in the vision. Leading up to a special day, our church family will knock on tens of thousands of doors throughout our community, inviting people and sharing the gospel with them. Many are saved in their homes and workplaces during this intense canvassing and soulwinning.

Praying for power—My favorite aspect of special days is the Saturday all-church prayer the evening before the special day.

What a thrill that Saturday night to see several hundred people gather for prayer. They pray for their pastor, for the visitors, and that God would work in the services in a wonderful way. James 4:2 reminds us, "ye have not, because ye ask not."

Biblical preaching—We often do a lot of special things on a special Sunday. Some of these may include a video presentation of the church ministry, themed decorations around the property, or new choir songs. But the central theme of the day is always the preaching of God's Word.

It's an amazing joy to watch as the Holy Spirit works and people respond to the gospel. To see the aisles filled with lost sinners coming to the Saviour is a thrill beyond any earthly joy.

Serving others—Another great aspect of a special day is watching our church family serve. Often, this includes serving hundreds of meals to guests. It is a blessing to me to see our members pouring drinks, serving meals, and taking time to meet the needs of others. And it binds our church family together in a special way.

Souls saved—How do you put a price on a single soul? I thank God for the conscientious soulwinners who take the time to share, verse by verse, the truth of the gospel. I thank God for the work of the Holy Spirit who brings conviction and new life to those who seek Christ. As I said earlier, we see people saved during the week leading up to our special event, during the services, and often during the meal following the services.

Joy—There is truly joy in serving Jesus! At the end of the day, I'm always tired, as are many of our church family who have been serving. But it is a deeply satisfied tired that rejoices to know that God uses us. There is always great joy in serving the Lord Jesus Christ!

LABORERS TOGETHER WITH GOD

To say that preparing for special days is easy would be terribly misleading. Actually, the planning, preparation, and sheer volume of soulwinning that is invested in these days is enormous. Yet, these days are incredibly rewarding.

Through special days, we seek out opportunities to facilitate the spread of the gospel. The labor is intense, but it is a privilege because we are "labourers together with God" (1 Corinthians 3:9).

From our first special day when we had 101 in church—double our average attendance—to our most recent special day when the Lord once again did exceeding, abundantly above our expectations, I don't regret one moment of time or one ounce of energy invested in staging opportunities to lead people to Christ. In our next chapter, we'll see the vital ingredient that should bind every aspect of our witness for Christ and to the lost—love. And we'll see that love really does work!

1　The notes in this chapter are prepared for soulwinners. For notes and checklists on the logistical aspects of scheduling and preparing for a special day, see chapters 18–19 in *Order in the Church* (Striving Together Publications, 2004).

2　Striving Together Publications offers a full-color brochure that carefully communicates the scriptural importance of baptism to a new convert. These are available in both English and Spanish.

FIFTEEN
LOVE WORKS!

For years, it has been my prayer that no honest history of the Antelope Valley of Southern California could be written without including the impact made by Lancaster Baptist Church. I want our church to so touch lives for Christ that we would see lives transformed by the power of the gospel and in turn affect the community where we minister.

Several months ago, we followed what we believed was the Lord's direction to help us get the gospel into our community in more venues than ever before by integrating a concept that was introduced by my son and our youth pastor, Larry, into our fall season of soulwinning. We called this forty-day outreach initiative "Love Works!" And did it ever work!

When we began the Love Works outreach, we weren't sure what the response would be. After twenty-seven years of our fall outreach being doorknocking alone, it was exciting to see what would happen when we combined doorknocking with serving our community. In a word, the response was *incredible*. What we saw in those six weeks confirmed in my heart the importance of touching lives with the love of Christ as we share the gospel.

The power of love is nothing we didn't already know. For years our church has ministered to the "unlovely," and for years, we have sought to go soulwinning with the compassion of Christ. What was so significant, however, about the Love Works program was how it forged a connection in the hearts and minds of people all across our community between the love of Christ and the gospel of Christ.

You see, sometimes in our care to avoid the social gospel which only addresses physical needs, we completely—and mistakenly—avoid being relational. It's hard to reach lives we do not touch. We can tell our communities that we love them, but if we are never willing to invest ourselves into their lives, our "love" will probably not be effective in leading people to Christ.

As we come to the end of this book, I'd like to challenge you to find practical ways to infuse your witness for Christ with the love of Christ. I'll share with you opportunities the Lord has given to our church, and hopefully you can incorporate some of these in your personal witnessing and even in your church soulwinning program.

But first, let's look at a backdrop for the scriptural directive to showing love—the parable of the Good Samaritan.

LOVE YOUR NEIGHBOR

You know the story of the Good Samaritan. You probably know the cast too—a wounded traveler, a priest, a Levite, and a Samaritan. The traveler was robbed, beaten, and left for dead. When the priest and the Levite came upon the scene, they carefully passed by on the other side of the road. Although they were religious leaders, they neglected their responsibility to love their neighbor. The Samaritan, however, was different. With a compassion we tend to avoid because it is inconvenient and costly, he rolled up his sleeves and demonstrated tangible love.

When we read or teach this parable, we tend to identify ourselves (or our neighbor) with one of the four cast players. We scorn the priest and the Levite and strive to be like the Good Samaritan. This, of course, was the point of Jesus' story. His exact words were "go and do thou likewise."

But, often we forget to whom Jesus was speaking…and how much we resemble His audience that day.

PHILOSOPHICAL COMPASSION

Luke 10 records more than a parable; it tells about the lawyer who prompted the parable. When this lawyer asked Christ how to inherit eternal life, his was not a "What must I do to be saved?" kind of question. It was a trap.

A first-century Jewish lawyer was not our stereotypical lawyer of the twenty-first century. He was a priest who interpreted the law and knew the Old Testament inside and out. He was playing word games with the Lord.

But Jesus wasn't easily trapped; He turned the question back to the lawyer and let him answer his own question. "What is written in the law? how readest thou?"

This lawyer knew the greatest commandment—the command to love God—so well that he quoted it word perfect: "And he answering said, Thou shalt love the Lord thy God with all thy heart, and with all thy soul, and with all thy strength, and with all thy mind; and thy neighbour as thyself" (Luke 10:27).

Through his own quoting of the law, particularly the phrase "and thy neighbour as thyself," the lawyer was convicted of his guilt. He knew he didn't love his neighbor. Unwilling to own up to the guilt, he attempted to justify himself with a fresh question: "And who is my neighbor?"

With those five words, the lawyer echoed our propensity— the bent to philosophize compassion.

Obviously, he wasn't asking who his neighbor was because he was overflowing with the desire to help, wondering on whom he could lavish his services. He wanted, rather, to abdicate himself of responsibility. His question spoke volumes: "I can quote the law, and I can give you theologically sound answers. But when it comes to actually showing compassion on someone, I'd rather just talk about the nuances of the law than get involved."

This is the context in which Jesus gave the parable of the Good Samaritan. Speaking to a man who wanted to excuse himself of the responsibility of love, Jesus got to the heart of compassion—action.

Too often, you and I are like that lawyer. We can recite the words, but we fail to live them. We understand the Bible, but we neglect to implement it. In short, we philosophize compassion.

We are *surrounded* by needs. We live in neighborhoods and communities desperate to see the love of God. And what is our response? We discuss the needs rather than rolling up our sleeves and meeting them. We want to talk about outreach, and we may even know the best ways to make it happen, but we don't actually touch lives. Like the lawyer, we've learned that it is easier to justify ourselves than it is to sacrifice. We know the story of the Good Samaritan, but we somehow miss the center message—*show the love of God.*

PUTTING SHOES ON LOVE

The Samaritan realized that love works. It doesn't just talk; it labors. When the Samaritan saw a need, he did not stand and stare. He did not rationalize the problem, and he did not ignore it. He took action.

In this, the Samaritan was like Christ. Jesus did more than look pityingly on us—He came to us. He did more than feel for hurting, broken people—He touched them and spent time with them. He did more than pray for the untouchables of society—He inconvenienced Himself to give long, grueling days ministering to them. He healed. He taught. He served. He gave.

From a humble birth in Bethlehem to His ultimate death on the cross, our Saviour demonstrated for us the greatest compassion of all when He gave His life for us. The Apostle John told us if we have the love of God, we will likewise lay down our lives for others: "Hereby perceive we the love of God, because he laid down his life for us: and we ought to lay down our lives for the brethren. But whoso hath this world's good, and seeth his brother have need, and shutteth up his bowels of compassion from him, how dwelleth the love of God in him? My little children, let us not love in word, neither in tongue; but in deed and in truth" (1 John 3:16–18).

Christlike compassion does not simply reside in our heads or our hearts. It affects our hands and our feet every time.

The Samaritan demonstrated the reality of his love by looking beyond social prejudice—which was as prevalent in the first century as it is in the twenty-first century. The Jews hated the Samaritans, and the feeling was mutual. For insight into the social atmosphere in the time of Jesus, listen to a Samaritan woman's statement from John 4:9: "Then saith the woman of Samaria unto him, How is it thou, being a Jew, askest drink of me, which am a woman of Samaria? For the Jews have no dealings with the Samaritans."

I believe Jesus purposefully addressed prejudice when He cast a Samaritan as the hero of His parable. The Samaritan was not only the hero, but he was the hero for a Jewish man. Of course, the Samaritan understood the victim was a Jew, but he helped anyway. He looked beyond social prejudice.

It's not politically correct today to admit prejudice, so we don't. But that doesn't mean we never deal with it. Whether it be based on color, lifestyle, or station in life, prejudice runs absolutely against Christlike love.

Do you want to know if your witness is tainted with prejudice? Look back over the past weeks in your ministry to people. Do you minister to people "on both sides of the tracks"? Do you serve every sector of your community? What have you intentionally done to show love to those who are "different than you" and to engage them with the gospel?

The compassionate love of God in the Samaritan's life was larger than cultural, man-made obstructions. To the Samaritan, the man in need was not an enemy, an outcast, or a threat; he was simply his neighbor.

The Samaritan proved his love with sacrifice. You don't have to have a college degree, deep resources, or special skills to show love. You just have to do it. Through the parable of the Good Samaritan, Jesus made it simple and practical. By rescuing the man, paying for his lodging, and ensuring continued care, the Samaritan gave his time, energy, resources, finances, and even his social reputation.

I often remind our church family that ministry that costs nothing accomplishes nothing. The reverse is also true. The more we are willing to sacrifice and the greater our love for God and others, the stronger our impact will be on a lost world. "For ye know the grace of our Lord Jesus Christ, that, though he was rich, yet for your sakes he became poor, that ye through his poverty might be rich" (2 Corinthians 8:9).

Yes, showing love costs. It is inconvenient and difficult. But if you haven't sacrificed, you probably haven't loved. When Jesus told the philosophical lawyer, "Love thy neighbor as thyself," He wasn't speaking of just *saying* "I love you." And He wasn't speaking of only showing love to people just like him. He was speaking of putting shoes on love—of making love work in real and practical ways toward people who may be difficult to love.

HOW LOVE WORKS

Christ's command, "Love thy neighbor as thyself," was the underlying premise of our Love Works program. The best way we can love our neighbors is by sharing the gospel with them. And in some cases—the cases we targeted through the Love Works program—the best way we can gain our neighbor's ear is by demonstrating love in a tangible way.

Here were our three objectives:

1. Express the love of God through works of kindness and compassion. We did this by going to rescue missions, public schools, public servant offices, hospitals—everywhere we could gain entrance to express the love of God.

2. Share the gospel of Christ with as many people as possible. Every act of kindness was accompanied with the gospel or with something that directed the recipient to the gospel. Even during the Love Works program, we continued our regular doorknocking efforts, and we found many opportunities to share the gospel with people as we completed various acts of service.

3. Impact our community as a church family. Matthew 5:16 instructs, "Let your light so shine before men, that they may see your good works, and glorify your Father which is in heaven." Through Love Works, we created opportunities to let our light shine as we worked to saturate the public venues of our community with expressions of God's love while at the same time we were taking the gospel message to every home.

PRACTICAL CONSIDERATIONS

So what went into this program in terms of preparation? Here are five steps you can follow:

1. Identify venues. We began by identifying every public service venue we could think of. Our list included the following:

- **Public schools**—We served meals to teachers and to sports teams, and we washed windows and cleaned fields at area schools.
- **Rescue missions**—We prepared and served meals in homeless shelters throughout our community.
- **Local hospitals**—We provided items to the victims unit and visited in the pediatric unit.
- **Commuter stations**—Because of our relative proximity to Los Angeles, many from our community travel back and forth on a daily basis. We went to the commuter stations (train and carpool) and served coffee and donuts from 4:00–6:00 AM. We served cookies and water as commuters returned in the evening.
- **Public servants' offices**—We provided and hosted barbecues and catered meals at local police and fire stations.
- **Public parks**—We painted, cleaned, and did repair work at city parks.
- **Local college**—We passed out free water and Gatorade to students on the local college campus.

We added more as well. Our church orchestra put on a free concert on the city square during our weekly Farmer's Market, while others gave out hot dogs and lemonade. We cleaned vacant lots and planted flowers outside nursing homes. All in all, we looked for every public venue where we thought we could create an opportunity to serve.

Additionally, we encouraged our church family to create their own opportunities—baking for their neighbors, paying it forward at a restaurant or drive-through, etc. The idea was to demonstrate Christian love to as many people in as many ways as possible.

2. Secure permissions. Obviously, you can't just take your barbecue grill to the local sheriff's station without asking permission first! As we planned out venues, we worked to secure permission through the proper channels before we began the program.

3. Build teams. Once we had most of the background work done, I shared the program with our church family. We created a website (loveworksav.com) through which members could sign up for projects. Additionally, each adult Bible class was assigned one or more projects, and many people worked with their classes to complete projects.

4. Execute thoroughly. We planned everything we could in advance—from ordering supplies to making sure we had plenty of gospel tracts ready at each event. We also gave every participant a blue t-shirt that said "Love Works" on the front and had our church website on the back. It was a good way to identify the acts of service with our church—to serve in Christ's name rather than in our own names.

5. Present the gospel. This was not a social gospel program. It was an emphasis on connecting relationally to share verbally the powerful gospel of Christ. We were not able to present the full plan of salvation with each person we talked to, but we were careful to include a gospel tract or invitation to our church.

From the earliest projects, we began seeing the fruit of souls saved. The very first week, people were saved on the spot in some of the venues including seven teens saved at a local high school and others saved at the rescue mission and through personal visits. Six weeks later, the responses to the gospel had been astounding.

After a month of the Love Works program, we hosted a "Love Works Sunday" on the week that would typically have been our Open House Sunday. Right from the outset of the acts of service, we had been inviting people to come to Love Works Sunday and to the complimentary "neighborhood barbecue" we would be hosting after the service.

The day before Love Works Sunday, we conducted our annual church-wide Saturday soulwinning, when we asked *all* of our soulwinners, regardless of what day they normally went out, to join together in a massive effort to complete the fall efforts of knocking on every home in our valley. This year, there was an even better than usual response as many people connected the soulwinners on their doorstep with the acts of service they had seen throughout the community over the previous weeks.

The response on Love Works Sunday was incredible. Hundreds of people who had been touched through the acts of service were our guests that Sunday, and many of them were saved. Even now, months later, we're seeing continuing fruit from the impact Love Works had in our community.

RESULTS OF LOVE THAT WORKS

If there was one truth that was confirmed in our hearts through the Love Works program it was that love is effective in reaching hearts. How?

God's love worked in creating evangelism opportunities. After serving public school teenagers in a variety of venues, some of our youth workers were able to personally lead several teens to Christ. Others were saved at the rescue mission, and more were saved in other venues. All of these are people who we are not as likely to reach through our usual doorknocking efforts, but the Love Works projects connected us with them in a way that opened opportunities to share the gospel.

God's love worked in fostering gospel-driven relationships. The Christian is to be a steward of the gospel in every relationship of life. But sometimes in our busyness we neglect to nurture relational gospel conversations with our neighbors and coworkers. One of the exciting parts of Love Works was watching our church family think of creative ways to show love to neighbors and coworkers in the name of Christ. Many shared with me how these acts of kindness gave them opportunity to lead a neighbor or coworker to the Lord!

God's love worked in impacting our community. Through Love Works, we were able to impact our community in a definite and Christ-honoring way. With gospel brochures, we served over 1,200 meals to the homeless, 500 cold drinks to students at Antelope Valley College, 100 meals to local high school sports teams, 1,800 hot dogs and lemonades at the Farmer's Market, 2,500 snacks to commuters at metro stations, and picked up trash from over 100 acres of vacant lots. And all of this made a definite impact.

God's love worked in soulwinning. As I already mentioned, every Love Works project was accompanied by the gospel, and we continued our usual doorknocking. Many of us noticed a warmer response to the doorknocking as people in our community had seen God's love displayed through our church in recent days. As is the case every year, our church family was able to lead many to the Lord out on doorsteps, even before the Love Works Sunday.

God's love worked in response to the gospel. On Love Works Sunday, I preached the gospel—the death, burial, and resurrection of Jesus Christ. I invited people to receive the gift of God's love and personally trust Christ as their Saviour. The response was overwhelming as scores of people were saved. Christ's love works! The love of God softens hearts to receive the gift of God!

Yes, God's love worked! And to God be the glory! We praise Him for every life He allowed us to touch with His love and for every soul saved as a result of sharing His love.

What about you? I'd challenge you to consider the people around you who you are praying to reach with the gospel—perhaps neighbors, coworkers, or even your entire community. Are you employing love in your efforts? Working love does work!

THE LEAST OF THESE

Understand, however, that the command to love our neighbors shouldn't be confined to a six-week program. While we cannot physically sustain year-round the level of investment that we committed during the Love Works program, the love of Christ should be embedded in our church ministries. Delivering the gospel with love is a biblical philosophy, not merely a program.

What does this look like practically? It includes serving those who are perhaps the unlovable members of society—who cannot repay our investments. In Matthew 25:40, Christ tells us that He cares deeply for "the least of these": "And the King shall answer and say unto them, Verily I say unto you, Inasmuch as ye have done it unto one of the least of these my brethren, ye have done it unto me."

To obey the Great Commission, we must "preach the gospel to every creature" (Mark 16:15). This includes every sector of our society—including the underprivileged, the "unlovely," and those who cannot repay. Actually, James 1:27 tells us we are to *especially* reach those who are the most needy. In one of the most heart-searching verses of the Bible, God tells us, "Pure religion and undefiled before God and the Father is this, To visit the fatherless and widows in their affliction, and to keep himself unspotted from the world" (James 1:27).

PURE RELIGION

"Pure religion" is not about building a "moral majority" in the culture…or saying "amen" in church. It's not just putting in time to go out soulwinning for the sake of a weekly duty. It is touching people where they are with the love of Christ. It is ministry that makes a difference in lives.

Obviously, this ministry must be accompanied with biblical integrity. James 1:27 even includes this principle in the phrase "to keep himself unspotted from the world." We can't neglect personal consecration and holiness to serve. We can't throw out discretion and Christian separation to impact people. After all, without the holiness of God embedded in our lives and in our message, what message would we be reaching people with anyway? We may communicate the gospel to them, but we would have a hard time discipling those young Christians in becoming Christlike in their lifestyle.

While we cannot compromise our message, neither can we neglect to carry our message with love. Remember, truth without love does not touch hearts. We can be completely "unspotted from the world" (which is good), but if we neglect to "visit the fatherless and widows in their affliction," we haven't shown Christ's love.

One of the most practical ministries through which to demonstrate Christ's love to "the least of these" is the bus ministry. Our church has conducted a bus ministry for twenty-six years now, and we have seen literally hundreds of children—most of whom have been from underprivileged, often shattered, homes—trust Christ as their Saviour.

Because the bus ministry is primarily directed toward children, the long-term fruit takes years to develop. Now, however, after twenty-six years of bus ministry, we are seeing the fruit of children who rode the church bus and trusted Christ as their Saviour break out of the embedded family patterns of their youth and live their adult lives for the Lord. One of these "bus kids" now pastors an extension chapel (an early church plant) of our church in a nearby city.

A few years ago, a school teacher in Los Angeles sent our ministry an email that further confirmed the far-reaching impact of the bus ministry:

> I am an English instructor at Roosevelt High School in Los Angeles. This past week, I assigned the writing of a speech celebrating Valentine's Day. One student, named Kevin, wrote a remarkable essay about your church.
>
> Kevin spoke of a "bus captain" named Brother Andrew…I have paraphrased the speech below. It stirred my heart, as a Christian, and caused several students to speak with Kevin about his faith.
>
> *Today I want to speak to everyone on what I think is true love. Love is not a movie or a feeling or an emotion. Love is God. I used to live in Palmdale with my family. There was a church there called Lancaster Baptist. The church sent buses out to pick up people in our apartment complex and take us to their church.*
>
> *Brother Andrew was my bus captain. Andrew was my friend; he showed me for the first time what it felt like to be really loved. My parents left my family when I was eleven, so we lived with my uncle there in Palmdale. Andrew told me that I still needed to love and talk to God about my parents, even though they had hurt me.*
>
> *Andrew always told me that he loved me, but he could never love me anywhere close to as much as God did. God loved me so much that he came to earth as a human named Jesus. Jesus died for all of us. How many of your boyfriends or girlfriends would really do that for you? Is that really love? No, it is not. Love is what I saw on that bus….*
>
> *Andrew would come to our apartment two or three times a week just to talk or hang out. He would*

come and talk to my uncle about Jesus and they would talk for hours about how to stop drinking and messing around with girls. Andrew would come get us after school, and we would go to the park or grab some food.

Andrew had no responsibility or reason to do any of this. He told me of a church and a pastor named Pastor Chappell that loved me. They would give of their money to run the buses. That is true love. Why would they love us kids like that? Because they wanted to tell us of a much bigger love, the love of God….

I understand that kids like Kevin don't meet the marketing paradigm of many churches today. Yet they need the gospel, and they respond to love.

My wife, Terrie, was saved through the bus ministry. It was promises of candy that brought her on the bus, but it was the kindness of the bus workers that brought her to the Lord. She was saved the second Sunday she rode the bus, and she continued to ride faithfully for years. Her heart for God, early Christian growth, and surrender of her life to the Lord was nurtured by the love and mentoring of bus workers.

There are other "Kevins" and "Terries" in the world. Many of them live in your city. What are you doing to reach them with the love of Christ?

CREATIVELY ENGAGING PEOPLE

I pray that this book has given you both motivation and instruction in reaching your community with the gospel of Christ. I pray it has reminded you of the urgency of Christ's command while at the same time providing practical "how to" instructions to obey His command.

Remember, however, that soulwinning isn't merely a program that is accomplished by reciting a script. Simply put, soulwinning is accomplished when Spirit-filled Christians engage lost people with the gospel message.

In these pages, I've shared with you the best ways I know to biblically engage people with the gospel—door-to-door soulwinning, relationship building, and love-driven service. Now I want to challenge you to find creative expressions of love as you use these principles to reach people with the gospel.

What does gospel creativity look like? It may be a single mom's oil change (we've seen several moms saved through this outreach!), delivering Thanksgiving meals to needy homes in your community, or taking "religious surveys" as you knock on the doors in your community yet another time. The possibilities are endless! But they do require creativity and love—and, most of all, the Word of God. Romans 10:17 says, "So then faith cometh by hearing, and hearing by the word of God."

A MESSAGE WORTH EVERYTHING

When Christ came to Earth, He gave everything. Why? Because He loves us.

If we are going to make His gospel known, we will have to give something. Time, energy, planning, care, love—soulwinning isn't cheap. But we have a message worth the sacrifice.

When we love Christ as we ought to and when we love our neighbors as He has commanded us to, we *will* share the gospel with others. And we will do it with the love that touches hearts and lives. Love still works!

CONCLUSION
IN COMMISSION

Whenever I have opportunity to visit my son and his wife and my granddaughter (especially my granddaughter) in San Diego, California, I go. Sometimes Matt and I will go for breakfast to the Harbor House Restaurant on the San Diego Bay.

Looking across the bay from the restaurant, you can see Point Loma Peninsula, home to several of our military installations, including a naval base. Matt and I sometimes look together at the mighty aircraft carriers in the bay waters. Although not as visible from a distance, Point Loma also hosts a squadron of submarines. By maintaining an aggressive operational schedule, including periodic deployment, these vessels are kept in absolute preparedness.

The aircraft carriers and submarines across the bay leave no question in your mind regarding the effectiveness and strength of our military.

But if you were to drive from San Diego eight hours north up Interstate 5, head a bit west on I-580 and then north on I-680, you'll cross the Benicia Bridge, which spans the Suisun Bay, home to another fleet of United States military vessels.

This scene, however, is very different from the scene in San Diego. It seems there is always a heavy, gray fog enshrouding the fleet you see from the bridge—the mothball fleet.

The contorted, rusted-out ship skeletons you can see through the mist are remnants of what *used* to be. These vessels were the heroes of World War II naval battles, but today they disintegrate in the bay waters—completely out of commission.

The contrast between Point Loma in San Diego and Suisun Bay in San Francisco is striking. One location maintains fleets of vessels capable of immediate military action with astounding power. The other is a dumping ground for abandoned, neglected vessels that once performed great feats of military prowess.

What is the difference? Upkeep.

The vessels in San Diego are maintained, while the vessels in San Francisco have been neglected.

Could I ask, which fleet of ships most closely resembles your witness for Christ? Are you prepared and ready, regularly sharing the gospel with the lost? Or are you rusty in your witness, rarely sharing God's offer of salvation?

If you are a pastor, take this question one step further and ask which fleet most closely resembles your church's witness for Christ. Is your church aggressive in saturating your community with the gospel, actively reaching the lost? Or is it burdened by programs and distracted with an inward focus so that it is slowly disintegrating, only resembling the great church it may have been at one time?

For both churches and individuals, when it comes to our level of engagement in sharing the gospel, we can't afford to begin tomorrow. *Delay* and *neglect* too easily become synonyms. We must engage today.

We've looked at the mothball fleet in Suisun Bay, but consider briefly the young men who once manned these vessels… and the tragic event that drew out their patriotism and courage.

Every American knows the date December 7, 1941, a date which President Franklin Roosevelt declared "will live in infamy." At 7:48 AM (Hawaiian Time), the United States was hurled into World War II by a surprise attack on our navy fleet in Pearl Harbor. To this day, historians argue aspects of the attack—including whether or not high ranking officials knew of it and failed to give warning. But no one argues the significance of the day, and no one wants to forget it either.

Few Americans, however, are aware of what happened on December 8—the day after the attack on Pearl Harbor. While December 7 may have been the definitive point of taking us into World War II, without December 8 we could not have successfully engaged in World War II.

So what is the significance of December 8? On that single day, the United States armed forces had more enlistments than any other day in American history—before or since.

> Nationwide, recruiting offices were flooded with applications for all three branches. Young boys of

> 'teen age' and grizzled veterans of the last war—
> swamped Army, Navy, and Marine recruiting
> stations here today....The recruiting office of the
> navy in Washington usually had three applicants on
> an average morning, but this morning, two hundred
> young men showed up. The phones of recruiting
> offices across the country began ringing...[1]

Consider the significance of the flood of young recruits. Many of these men had just been through the Great Depression. They had seen little of the promise and opportunity of America but had known privation, frustration, and hardship. Yet, when their country needed them, they were all in—immediately and willingly. When urgency was upon them, they responded without hesitation.

When it comes to the Great Commission Christ has given us, urgency is upon *us*. We live in a day of unprecedented spiritual warfare. Marriage is being redefined, Christians in oppressive countries are being more persecuted than ever before,[2] and even in America freedoms for Christians are being undermined in the name of a dangerous "tolerance."

All throughout Scripture, God attaches an urgency to salvation and preaching the gospel. Second Corinthians 6:2 says, "...behold, *now* is the accepted time; behold, *now* is the day of salvation." Christ told His disciples, "Lift up your eyes, and look on the fields; for they are white *already* to harvest" (John 4:35).

May we sense the urgency today to enlist ourselves and to reengage our efforts in the greatest commission on Earth—delivering the gospel to a lost world. May we sense this urgency *before* a moral atomic bomb drops, *before* our freedoms to publicly preach the gospel are taken. May we carefully examine our witness and do whatever is necessary to engage fully in what Christ has commissioned us to do.

Through these pages, we've taken a good, hard look at needed repairs to get us back to obeying the Great Commission. We've "lifted the hood" to examine the engine. We've noted practical steps to get back on track. And we've looked at creative ideas for moving forward.

Before you turn this last page and close this book, however, I'd like to challenge you with one final question: *Are you in commission?*

---

1   Craig Shirley, *December 1941: 31 Days that Changed America and Saved the World* (Thomas Nelson, Inc., 2011), 171.

2   Joshua Rhett Miller, "Christians Killed for Faith Nearly Doubled in 2013, Group Finds" (January 12, 2014), http://www.foxnews.com/world/2014/01/12/christians-killed-for-faith-nearly-doubled-in-2013-group-finds/.

ABOUT THE AUTHOR

PAUL CHAPPELL is the senior pastor of Lancaster Baptist Church and president of West Coast Baptist College in Lancaster, California. His biblical vision has led the church to become one of the most dynamic Baptist churches in the nation. His preaching is heard on Daily in the Word, a daily radio broadcast heard across America. Pastor Chappell has four children who are married and serving in Christian ministry. He has been married to his wife Terrie for over thirty years, and they have four married children and five grandchildren. His children are all serving in Christian ministry.

You can connect with Dr. Chappell through his blog, Twitter, and Facebook:

paulchappell.com
twitter.com/paulchappell
facebook.com/pastor.paul.chappell

Visit us online

strivingtogether.com

wcbc.edu

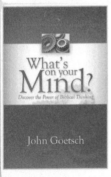